THE RELUCTANT EXORCIST

The Reluctant Exorcist

KEN GARDINER

KINGSWAY PUBLICATIONS
EASTBOURNE

ISBN 1 84291 074 4

Published by
KINGSWAY COMMUNICATIONS LTD
Lottbridge Drove, Eastbourne, BN23 6NT, England.
Email: books@kingsway.co.uk

Book design and production for the publishers by
Bookprint Creative Services, P.O. Box 827,
BN21 3YJ, England.
Printed in Great Britain.

Contents

Foreword

In our local bookshop the shelf marked 'Traditional Religions' is getting smaller, while the section marked 'Witchcraft' is expanding! In recent years there has been a number of newspaper reports on 'ritual' killings in this country and in Europe. As Christians it is easy to throw up our hands in despair, but can we read the signs of the times?

More and more people are recognising that our spiritual nature is not just something that is 'caught', but rather something deeply wired into each one of us. Many will testify that there is a spiritual vacuum in the hearts and minds of our nation today. As we know, nature abhors a vacuum and will rush to fill it. But how, and with what, will it be filled? If the Christian church in this new millennium does not or cannot rise to this challenge, then others will!

It has been my privilege to work alongside Canon Gardiner over a number of years. Ken is a man of deep faith and personal holiness, as well as someone who possesses a great deal of practical common sense and professional integrity. Therefore, Ken's book on the ministry of deliverance is a

Godsend. Speaking from years of experience as a parish priest within the Church of England, Ken takes us on a guided tour of this rather specialised ministry. Having stumbled into this work by accident, Ken assures his reader that he is no expert. Because, as he says, there are no experts in this field! What he can and does offer is experience – a wealth of experience that has guarded and guided him in the past 30 years. He rightly sees the ministry of deliverance firmly within the parochial setting. Ken speaks as one who is unashamedly from the evangelical/charismatic wing of the church, and yet having a deep respect for all who work in this area. Reading his many moving yet humorous case histories, one soon discovers Canon Gardiner's pastoral heart. Being person-centred, Ken sees his ministry as helping people to become whole in body, mind and spirit. To do this effectively, he advocates the ideal of working in partnership with the medical profession.

For those who have stumbled across paranormal activity in their ministry and wondered what on earth (and in heaven) to do, this is a useful book. For those who are experienced in this ministry, this is a challenging book. For those who can read the 'signs of the times' and wish to respond appropriately, this is an essential book.

The Ven. Norman Warren
Archdeacon Emeritus of Rochester

Introduction

When it comes to ministering in the realm of the occult, whether it be with regard to people or places, I do not believe there are any experts; it is just that some ministers have had more experience than others. In my own case it happened like this.

As an ordinary parish priest (who had not come to ordination until the age of 35, after a number of years first in the army and then in commerce), I was approached by a member of our congregation who told me that he felt he was under some form of demonic oppression. He was a very intelligent man, successful in one of the professions, and I could not dismiss his views lightly even had I wished to do so. However, I did not know what to do. I believe my ordination training was as good as any – and better than some – but, as far as I can recall, the occult had not been even mentioned, let alone included, in the curriculum. Like many people, I was aware that the realm existed, but I was at a loss when confronted with someone who was seeking my help in gaining relief.

Looking back, I now believe that it is scandalous that a

priest of the established church of the land should have been given no instruction at all about what, even 40 years ago, was a growing problem, following the repeal of the Witchcraft Act in 1951 and the selling of Ouija boards as a family game in toy shops (with the comment in the accompanying instructions that the 'player' must take the whole matter seriously if the 'game' is to work). I am not suggesting that every incumbent should be fully trained to minister in the realm of deliverance, but he should certainly be aware of the basics and instructed as to how and where he can obtain guidance – which, I am glad to report, is the case with regard to most dioceses today.

Some years after I was ordained, the then principal of my college asked previous students whether we felt there had been any omissions in our training. I mentioned this matter of the occult and he commented that it was totally a matter of the mind and should be dealt with by counselling – which *had* been covered in our training – or, in more extreme cases, by a qualified psychiatrist. This, he explained, was because evil spirits did not exist! I understand that the situation is a little better now, with a number of theological colleges including in their curriculum at the very least a reference to the existence of the paranormal and some guidance on where help may be found. Many dioceses, including my own, now provide every parish with a copy of 'Bishop's Instructions', which give details of whom to contact for advice in dealing with the occult.

With regard to the person who had approached me for help, I was aware that in a neighbouring parish there was a clergyman who had considerable experience of dealing with people who believed they were oppressed by evil spirits, and I turned to him for help. I will not describe here the details of the case, or how he dealt with it, because the procedure will be explained later. Suffice it to say that I learned a great deal from him.

Some time later, my bishop sent a letter to all incumbents to say that he had set up a group of three priests in the diocese who should be consulted regarding all cases of deliverance. I immediately wrote to advise him of the case of our parishioner and the apparently successful outcome. It so happened that shortly afterwards the Bishop of Exeter's Commission on Exorcism, which had recently published its report (1972), offered my bishop two places on a training seminar if he would like to nominate suitable candidates. He kindly offered one of the places to me, and I spent nearly a week with some very experienced members of the Commission, including Dom Robert Petitpierre OSB, the Chairman, the Revd John Richards, the Secretary, and Dr Ken McCall, a medical missionary who was also a qualified psychiatrist. Although it is impossible to gain full training in a week (and, as I have already stated, I do not believe there are any experts in this field), I was given an insight and grounding which has proved invaluable.

On my return, the bishop asked me to join the existing group of advisers for the diocese, and I have served on this group ever since – continuing into what is euphemistically described as retirement. Because of this, over the years I have been involved in a number of referrals and consequently I have gained a certain amount of experience. However, I am still learning, because no two cases are exactly the same.

Before sharing some of my observations and experiences, I must clarify a number of points. First, it is not an area of ministry I have ever sought, or one that I enjoy – although there is always the 'reward' of a successful outcome. Indeed, I find

I still come to every new 'case' with some apprehension. Second, and particularly with regard to dealing with people as distinct from places, I am reluctant to assume that the problem is demonic. In my experience, it is far more likely to be one that requires counselling rather than deliverance. Third, where there does seem to be some demonic oppression, I am very aware that I have no power or ability of my own. I do believe I have authority, but it is the authority given by our Lord Jesus Christ. The power, the victory and the glory are his alone. I am convinced that the greatest danger faced by those who minister in this realm is to forget that truth and to believe that he or she has some personal ability or gifting which enables them to succeed.

I hope it will not seem patronising if I commend the excellent book *Deliverance* published by SPCK (second edition 1996) and edited by Canon Michael Perry on behalf of the Christian Deliverance Study Group. This is the follow-up group to the original Commission set up by the Bishop of Exeter in 1964 to which I have already referred. I cannot hope to equal the scholarship and detailed research on which that book is based.

Why, then, have I written this book based solely on my experiences as one individual? There are a number of reasons: first, throughout *Deliverance* the point is made that while it would be totally wrong to ignore or misrepresent the facts of a case, the interpretation of those facts is open to differing opinions. With some hesitation, I confess that my own interpretation of the facts does differ from those of the group in respect of a few of their findings. I think that this is probably due, to some extent, to a difference in background. I come from an evangelical/charismatic stable and, while I have broadened my outlook considerably in the course of my ministry, my basic belief in the reliability of the Bible, its careful differentiation between sickness and demonisation, and the way Jesus, Paul and others cast out evil spirits, is something that colours my thinking, and my personal experience confirms it.

The second reason is akin to that. The approach of the Christian Deliverance Study Group is from a moderate to High-Church perspective, with a leaning towards liturgy and ritual – there is an appendix to their book giving suggested forms of prayer. The editor is careful to explain that these are not to be regarded as magical incantations, and that the thoughts contained in them may be expressed by the minister in his own words. Nevertheless, useful as this material is, I know my evangelical colleagues too well not to realise that many of them will be wary of this approach, and the references to holy water and requiems for the departed may cause some of them to dismiss much of the book without 'reinterpreting' the very real truths within it into terms more familiar to their brand of churchmanship.

Some years ago, I attended a meeting arranged within our diocese as an introduction to the subject of the occult from a Christian perspective. The speaker was a member of the Christian Deliverance Study Group and from a High-Church tradition but, unknown to him, about three-quarters of his audience were evangelicals – the majority of them lay leaders. Some of the things he said I would have expressed differently, due to my background, and this would probably have been more acceptable to his audience. However, there was only one point he made with which I seriously disagreed. Unfortunately, many at the meeting took such exception to this particular statement that I believe they did not really hear much of the useful material he did share. Hopefully, the fact that I come to this subject from the perspective of an evangelical and a charismatic, yet as a priest firmly within the Anglican tradition, may help to overcome unnecessary prejudice against the particular approach set out in Canon Perry's book. I would mention in particular that I find the chapter about 'casualties' of attempted exorcism, contributed by the present Bishop of Reading, the Rt Revd Dominic Walker, in which he refers at some length to the contribution made by charismatics but warns against their excesses, is generous as well as a careful and timely warning.

God is too big for any group within any denomination to have all the truth about him. There are more ways than one of dealing with the paranormal. The essential truth for those engaged in this ministry is whether we know that we come in the name of the Lord Jesus Christ; if we are certain of that, then the powers in the unseen but very real spiritual realm seem to be aware of it also. They may have no fear of us, but they know they have to yield before him who on the cross triumphed over all powers and authorities (Colossians 2:15).

In the illustrative cases included in this book, names and certain details have been changed to preserve confidentiality, but the events described are all true.

1
The Cleansing of Places

A word of explanation

The term 'exorcism' is often used to describe both the freeing of people and the ridding of places from demonic activity. Some people hold that exorcism should strictly be applied only when talking about people. Because of the hype encouraged by some sections of the media, I prefer to avoid the term exorcism as being too sensational, and I find it more helpful to speak of the deliverance of people and the cleansing of places. Both have to do with the occult.

The word 'occult' simply means 'hidden', and has come to refer to the mysterious happenings which at present have no scientific explanation. The term is normally used to cover such things as astrology, fortune-telling, horoscopes, tarot cards, divining with runes, automatic writing, using a Ouija board (or glass moving), consulting mediums or spiritists, witchcraft, black magic and Satanism. In short, it is any means of seeking paranormal guidance or power from a source other than God. Some would therefore extend this list to embrace such things as extrasensory perception (ESP), water or metal dowsing and some forms of alternative medicine such as acupuncture, homeopathy, reflexology and the like.

A Ouija board (the word means 'yes' in French and German) is usually heart-shaped, having ball-bearings placed on the under side. The letters of the alphabet are spread on a table in a circle or semicircle; the participants place their fingers lightly on the board and questions are asked of the 'spirit'. The board moves and the point of the heart indicates different letters, spelling out the answer. Very often the same effect is obtained by the fingers being placed on an upturned glass, which moves from letter to letter.

At once we face the question: is there really a power behind the occult, or is it some form of psychological deception? There is little doubt that in many instances there is the release of some force or energy; objects move, apparently by themselves, and sounds and smells are produced. However, does that energy come from some outside source, or is it produced unconsciously in some way by the people who experience the phenomena? And, if it is the latter, is the energy *used* by some outside influence or is it a manifestation of their own psyche?

Although it can be helpful to understand such phenomena and how they occur, the task of those of us involved in helping people who desire to be free of them is not primarily to research where they come from or what causes them, but to get rid of them. There have been many occasions when I have been unsure of what I have been dealing with but, following ministry, the manifestations have ceased. What may be useful is to discover the point of entry – what caused the manifestations to begin? Very often in dealing with places, and almost always when dealing with people, somebody has done something in the realm of the occult which opens the door to the unwanted presence or activity.

Occurrences of the paranormal in places and in people have certain similarities, but they are very different in their manifestation. I have found it helpful to keep the two separate in my mind and so I shall adopt this practice in this book, dealing first with places and then with people.

In the Church of England, bishops wisely seek to exercise some control over this rather specialised ministry, in order to curtail the insensitive approach of those who see demons everywhere and exorcise anyone and anything at the drop of a hat. I refer to it as a specialised ministry because, although I believe that it is, or ought to be, simply part of the task of all clergy in helping people to become whole, it has caused serious problems in the past when well-meaning but totally inexperienced people have sought to minister to others who may be in a disturbed mental or emotional state. In most dioceses the bishop has appointed people with some experience of this ministry to be his advisers. Cases of paranormal activity which arise in different parishes are referred to these advisers, who consequently gain more experience. Although this is useful because it builds up a store of information, almost every case is different in some respect from any other. There is so much that I do not understand, and I learn something new on almost every occasion.

Manifestations

It is important to understand that there is a variety of events springing from different sources, and these should not be confused. For instance, some are related to the past and others to the present.

Hauntings

People tell of strange apparitions – grey figures disappearing through solid walls, men or women in ancient dress gliding silently along corridors. Very often these are what I am happy to call a place memory. This is an event which really happened in the past, and often (but not always, so far as we can know) an event which generated strong emotion. It seems that something in the present triggers off a 'replay' of that event. It isn't actually happening again. The analogy falls down if taken too far, but it is rather like making a family video of a child learning to walk and then playing it back 20 years later.

There are stories of people who live near the scene of some great historical battle hearing sounds of clashing swords, neighing horses, etc. on a particular night of the year – usually the anniversary of the event. Very often, when people speak of seeing a ghost walking along a garden path and vanishing through a brick wall, it will transpire that years earlier there was a door in the wall at that point, which has since been bricked up.

I heard Dom Robert Petitpierre, who was Chairman of the Bishop of Exeter's Commission on Exorcism, tell the story of the owner of a large country house who had the experience of watching a hunt, complete with horses, riders and dogs, go through his billiard room in full cry! After this had happened on a number of occasions, the floor of the room was raised several feet. The next time the hunt went through, the riders were visible only from the waist up!

My own father told me of a strange event. He was churchwarden and organist with the Revd Dr Oesterley, a well-known Old Testament scholar at the beginning of the twentieth century. On one occasion, during the week when the church was empty, my father was in the church vestry when

Dr Oesterley came in, looking rather shaken. He explained that he had just seen the previous vicar of the church, dressed in clerical robes, walk down the aisle and out through the main door, which was shut. That vicar had loved the church dearly, but had moved to another parish in a different part of the country, where he was still alive and working, apparently totally unaware of his 'appearance' at his previous church.

One case on which I was consulted had some circumstances similar to a place memory, but important differences also. A clergyman telephoned to ask my advice. His mother had died a few months earlier, and his father was still living in the flat they had occupied together. This was situated in a large house, which had been converted into a number of separate flats with a common hall and staircase. A man who lived in one of the other flats, and who had known both the husband and the wife for some time, had come home and 'seen' very clearly the woman in the hall, looking distressed. The experience was so vivid that he had mentioned the matter to the husband, who had, in turn, told his son, who then personally questioned the man.

The clergyman was, naturally, concerned for his father; he was also uneasy at the thought that his dead mother might not be at peace but was tied to this earth in some way. I said that I believed this was most unlikely, but I explained the phenomenon of a 'place memory' and asked whether he knew of any occasion when his mother had undergone a traumatic experience in the hall. Immediately, he recalled that a few weeks before her death she had apparently gone into the hall during the night, where she had had a mild stroke. This had caused her to fall down, and she lay there all night until her husband woke in the morning and discovered her. I suggested that he should pray in the hall along the lines I will explain below.

What was unusual about this case is that while there had indeed been an event which must have caused emotional trauma, normally a 'place memory' is an exact replay of an event. However, here the mother was moving or standing normally when, in reality, she had fallen down and remained on the floor for several hours. This simply goes to prove that no two cases are exactly identical.

What triggers the 'place memory' to replay is a mystery. However, a simple prayer proclaiming the peace and presence of Christ over the area is usually enough to stop further manifestations. Some involved in this ministry may sprinkle holy water. I have come to the conclusion that there is no single method of cleansing that has to be used; much depends upon the tradition and churchmanship of the minister involved. I have used a variety of different methods from various traditions, as seem appropriate at the time. God is greater than we are, and he answers when we call on him to deal with the situation. I believe that when dealing with a 'place memory' there is no need to demand that some evil spirit should depart. Personally, I do not pray that the unhappy soul of the 'ghost' should be at peace, any more than I would pray when watching the family video of 20 years ago that the little child I am looking at would learn to walk. I do not believe that any 'soul' is there; it is just a 'memory'. However, if a minister thinks it is helpful to pray in such a way, no harm is being done.

Poltergeists

The name is made up of two German words, meaning 'noise' and 'spirit'; thus, it is a noisy spirit. A number of investigators of the paranormal, often those who would not claim any particular religious affiliation, believe that poltergeist activity is usually associated with the presence of young people around the age of puberty. That is not to say that these young people are deliberately or consciously causing it; it may be that in some way the poltergeist is able to draw on energy produced by such a person. I would not wish to refute this view. My task has never been scientific investigation, and my interest in the cause is only to the extent that it may help me to learn best how to get rid of the disturbance. I have to say that in my personal experience, which is not as wide as those who concentrate on investigating these matters, very rarely have I found that young people of that age live in the homes involved. In fact, often there are very young children, who may well be far more susceptible to active imagination, interpreting the sounds of central heating systems and expanding or contracting floorboards as the presence of ghosts or wicked goblins. I have found that these paranormal events occur in the homes of people of all ages, including the elderly who live on their own.

Personally, I do not find the term 'poltergeist' helpful, because manifestations take many different forms, some of which are totally silent. It will probably be helpful if I describe some of the disturbances I have met.

I remember being called to a bungalow occupied by three people, a husband and wife and the sister of one of them, all retired. A number of items of stationery were discovered on the floor or on chairs: paper-clips, drawing-pins, ordinary pins and the like. They had no idea how they got there, until on one occasion they noticed a paper-clip dropping from the ceiling. As they watched, other small items appeared, seemingly coming through the ceiling. They showed me a bowl of these items which they had collected. It had been going on for some considerable time but, because it was harmless, they had not bothered to do anything about it. Eventually, however, they decided that it was an unnecessary annoyance and contacted me, their local vicar, to see if I could do anything about it.

Of course, this description would not satisfy any scientific investigator of the paranormal – how can I be sure that these three people were telling the truth, or were not deluded? I have already said that I am not primarily interested in proving that paranormal activity genuinely exists – I wish it didn't. My concern is to get rid of it. My attitude is very simple: why should three perfectly ordinary adults bother to conspire together to pretend that some strange manifestations had occurred, and contact their parish priest to ask his help? What strange delight could they gain from fooling me in such a way?

A similar case related to larger items, tins or packets of food, which would mysteriously disappear from a cupboard, only to turn up in a house two or three doors further down the road. I cannot recall exactly how the people concerned discovered that the missing items had arrived at the other house; presumably they knew their neighbours and must have mentioned to them the strange and frequent disappearances, at which the neighbours would have remembered the equally strange arrival of items they had not purchased. This case was unusual in that movement of articles mostly occurs within the one house, and not between houses, particularly if there are other houses in between. Such manifestations as these are annoying and vaguely disturbing, but do not strike terror in the hearts of the people affected. However, there are manifestations that can be very frightening indeed.

The case of the sofa and the wardrobe

I remember a mother, with two young children in tow, turning up on my doorstep in a distressed state. There had been a number of incidents in her home when furniture had been moved. She had never actually witnessed the movement but had certainly heard it. On one occasion, she had heard a crash from a bedroom and had rushed up the stairs to discover that a wardrobe had fallen forward onto the floor. Her husband was away, working overseas, and she was living alone in the house with the two children. Things had been getting worse, with the paranormal activity increasing, and she had contacted a friend, who suggested that she come to see me and, in fact, accompanied her to my house. The woman was very frightened indeed and begged me to come with her to her home there and then. I did so and she led the way into her hall, opened the door into the front room and suddenly screamed. The sofa had been tipped forward completely so that its back and its bottom formed two sides of a triangle, pointing upwards. Obviously, much more force would have had to have been used to do this than if it had fallen on its back.

We inspected the rest of the house and found that there was one bedroom door which would not open because something had fallen against it. I applied my weight to the door and was able to push it open sufficiently for us to squeeze through. A wardrobe (the one that had previously crashed forward) had fallen at an angle against the door. I suppose it could be that the woman had up-ended the sofa before she came to me, and manipulated the wardrobe against the bedroom door so that it would fall sideways as she shut it behind her. Alternatively, some other person might have found a way to enter the house and do all this while she was out. Again, however, what is the point of such deception? When I left them and went home, were they laughing behind my back, saying to each other, 'That fooled the vicar'? If so, I am not bothered. However, I have no doubt at all that the woman was genuinely scared.

Such cases are obviously not 'place memories'. This is no replay of a past event which has no reality in the present. Material articles, sometimes very heavy articles, are moved about for no reason at all.

Gathering information

Before commencing any form of ministry, I question the people closely. Have they been involved with the occult in any way? I spell out what I mean – seeking to contact the dead or foretell the future, etc. I extend this to other members of the family, especially parents, because there can be an inheritance factor.

I enquire when the manifestations began, and probe to see if there was any change in family circumstances or behaviour at that time. I then ask about other possible manifestations which they have not mentioned, and which they may not realise could be associated with the incidents they have described. These might include a strange and usually distasteful smell in a particular area, or 'cold spots'. Very often people will refer to the fact that a particular room is always very cold, or there is an area (often on the stairs, but I have no idea why) where it is unnaturally cold.

I will ask if they have noticed any unusual occurrences relating to electrical items. It is very common for people to report lights turning on or off by themselves, and similar experiences with radios and television sets, or electric clocks stopping for no reason. I sometimes wonder if this frequent manifestation of electrical malfunction is in any way linked to the energy that must be required to move articles around; but, of course, I have no evidence of this.

I also enquire if there are any animals in the home and, if so, whether they have exhibited any strange behaviour. Cats, and especially dogs, react very strongly to an occult presence. Sometimes they will refuse to go into a particular room. Often dogs will behave as though they are looking at some unseen person; sometimes growling but, more often, cowering and frightened. On occasions I have actually seen their hair stand on end. Reactions like this from animals can be a great help in establishing whether or not there is some occult activity in the house. (When I come to the section dealing with the deliverance of people, I will recount the astonishing reaction of a budgerigar!)

I will ask about their neighbours, because I have known spiritist mediums practise in their own homes and for their neighbours to be affected. Often, however, people have no idea whether the people next door are involved in the occult or not.

When I have gathered all the information I can, I do my best to explain to the people who have asked for help what may have started the manifestation. If, as is often the case, one or more of them has been involved with the occult, I will read to them the following passage of Scripture:

> There shall not be found among you any one that maketh his son or his daughter to pass through the fire, or that useth divination, or an observer of times, or an enchanter, or a witch. Or a charmer, or a consulter with familiar spirits, or a wizard, or a necromancer. For all that do these things are an abomination unto the Lord: and because of these abominations the Lord thy God doth drive them out from before thee. Thou shalt be perfect with the Lord thy God. (Deuteronomy 18:10–13, KJV)

I always make certain that I have a Bible with me – usually a modern translation, although the above quotation is from the KJV – and I always read the passage aloud, because I am sure that this carries more weight than if I were to paraphrase it in my own words. I explain the meaning of any particular term which applies to the people involved. Thus 'divination' embraces those who attempt to discover the future by stars and horoscopes, and 'an observer of times' refers to those who believe that there are particularly propitious days when a task should or should not be undertaken. Enchanters and charmers are those who seek to interpret omens (cards, tea-leaves, etc.) or cast spells. A consulter with familiar spirits is a medium or spiritist, and a necromancer is one who consults the dead. Witches and wizards may well use any or all of these practices, plus various other occult activities.

Those who consult mediums are very often impressed because they receive a message which seems to confirm that they are, indeed, in contact with some relative who has died. For instance, they may be told to go into the loft and find a cardboard box which contains letters tied up with ribbon. They do this and do, in fact, discover such a box. 'Why,' they say, 'it must really be Granny giving that message because no one else could have known about it.' But what if there were spirits who were aware of many facts about Granny and were 'familiar' with her ways? I am not implying that they were necessarily attached to or within her – simply familiar with several things about her during her lifetime. These familiar spirits might very well convey such details through a medium and thus impersonate Granny in order to win converts to their cause and draw people away from the truth of God which is found in Jesus Christ.

A method of cleansing

I point out that because they have called on me, obviously they have some belief in God or, at least, they believe that as a priest of God I may be able to do something about their problem. I remind them of what I have just read from the Bible and explain that God is against whatever they have been doing in the occult realm. Before I go further, I ask if they agree that it is wrong. I find that this is essential. Later, I will ask them to repent of what they have done, but they cannot do this genuinely unless they have faced the fact that they have sinned against God and his Law, and it was not some harmless bit of fun.

I will then try to explain the situation in the spiritual realm with the following example from everyday life. 'Let's suppose,' I say, 'that you decide to invite a lodger into your home. After a while, you realise that he is causing problems, and you want him out. You withdraw the invitation and ask him to leave. That ought to be enough; he ought to go. However, if he doesn't, you may call the police to throw him out. The lodger may say that he has a right to stay because you invited him in. If the police ask if that is correct, you will say, "Yes, but I have now withdrawn the invitation and I have told him to leave." If he does not do so, the police can demand that he leave, because he is now a trespasser. That is very similar to what you have done,' I explain. 'You invited some spirit other than the Holy Spirit into your life. That was foolish and against God's Law. You must withdraw the invitation. I cannot do that for you; it was you who made the invitation and so you must withdraw it. Once you have done that, then I can act as a sort of spiritual policeman and command the thing, whatever it is, to go, because it is now trespassing.'

I find that people can relate to that illustration, and are willing to repent of their action. I then explain that I will say a prayer, after which I will say, 'Over to you.' Then, using their own words, they are to say briefly four things: first, that they did wrong in . . . (whatever it is – consulting a medium, playing with a Ouija board, etc.); second, that they are sorry; third, they ask God to forgive them; finally, they say that they will never do it again. I will go over those four things again, explaining in particular that there should be no excuses, just confession and repentance.

Most people are not used to praying aloud, which is why I pray first. I do this in a very gentle way, avoiding a false piety and using everyday language, sitting where we are. 'Father, we are your children and we come to you now, to say that Joan knows she has done wrong in playing with the Ouija board (or whatever) and she wants to tell you she is sorry and ask your forgiveness. Help her to find the words as she talks to you. All right, Joan, over to you. Just speak to God as you would to a friend.' I am constantly surprised at how easily the great majority of people pray aloud, even though they know that I am there listening to them. Hopefully, for some, this will be the start of a regular, natural prayer life, once they realise that you don't have to use a special, old-fashioned language. Very often, they will start making excuses without realising it: 'Lord, I am sorry I went to that medium; I didn't realise it was wrong; I just wanted to contact my gran and . . .' I have no hesitation in butting in gently and saying, 'Now, Joan, you are trying to explain why you did it. No excuses, just "sorry".' I find that this doesn't put them off, and it puts them back on track. If they have omitted any of the four, I will say, 'That was great, Joan, but you didn't actually promise that you will never do it again.' And in every case they are happy to finish their prayer as I have requested. I am sure that it is vital to create a normal and relaxed atmosphere, and then they have no problem with praying in this way.

Very rarely (I can recall only two occasions), the person

really has not been able to formulate a prayer themselves. In those cases, I asked them to repeat a prayer, phrase by phrase, after me. I believe it is important that they speak out the words themselves. They opened the door to whatever it is that is causing the problem, and it is they who must shut it.

I then close with a prayer along the lines of 'Thank you, Father, that you have heard Joan's prayer. Be with us now as we order this evil presence to leave this home. Keep Joan and all her family safe, and may she come to know you personally more and more as the days go by. Amen.'

I explain that now that she has withdrawn the invitation, so to speak, I can command the thing to go. If I have not already established the principal area where the manifestations occur, I will ask further questions, and then I will go to that room. I always ask the person to accompany me, together with anyone else of the family who is present at the time – especially any children, who may be frightened. (Sometimes a parent will deliberately ask me to call when the child is *not* there, because they judge that it will be unnecessarily disturbing to him or her. I respect their judgement.) The reason I ask them to accompany me is that I believe it helps if they actually hear the words I speak.

Even if I am not convinced that there *is* any occult activity, I work on the principle that if it is purely psychological, then the fact that they have called me in shows that they have some degree of belief that I can do something to help, and hearing me command the thing to go may be all they need for their psychological fear to dissipate. If there *is* some occult power involved, then the prayer will be effective, and it can give them confidence to have heard me. So whether the disturbance is real or imagined, they will benefit from hearing me pray.

On one occasion, when I was fairly new to this ministry, I

did all that I have explained above and prayed in the room (in this case, the only room) where the manifestation had occurred. A week later, I checked to see if all was well, and I was told that that room was perfectly clear but the manifestations had moved to other areas of the house. So I prayed in every other room, and there was no more trouble. I now don't waste time; I pray in every room from the outset – explaining to the family why I have found it sensible to do so.

In the area where the main manifestation has occurred, I will say something like, 'I come in the name of the Lord Jesus Christ, and I take authority over every spirit contrary to the Holy Spirit of God. In the name of the Lord Jesus, you are to leave this home; you are to hurt no one and you are to be subject to Jesus, never to afflict anyone or anything again. On the authority given to me by the Lord Jesus Christ, go, now!' I then go round every other room, including the bathroom and the toilet, the outhouse and the basement. Usually, with regard to attics and basements, I will pray at the foot or top of the stairs, unless they are regularly occupied as rooms. Almost always the person who accompanies me will say as we set out, 'I'm afraid it isn't very tidy,' and certainly, when we come to a teenager's room, it rarely is! I will reply in a relaxed manner, 'Oh, don't worry; surely you can be free in your own home' – anything to keep everything low-key.

Usually I say only one sentence in each room, perhaps as brief as, 'The peace of Christ be on all who sleep here,' or 'Jesus is Lord.' There are some priests who like to use a written and set form of prayer for cleansing. Some may sprinkle holy water, hold a cross or crucifix, or make the sign of the cross. I will very often do the latter on a door or a wall. Frankly, it is as I feel it right at the time. Let me say again, the minister should act in accordance with the way he feels most at ease;

God is greater than we are, and evil spirits seem to be very aware of what we are about. They know where our confidence lies and seem to sense whether we are trusting in ourselves or come as representatives of Christ. If *we* know it is the latter, they seem not to doubt it either, and they have to yield at his name. I will refer to this in greater detail under the subject of deliverance.

Before I leave, I explain that it is unlikely that they will have any further trouble (it is helpful to build up their confidence) but that it is just possible that the thing will have one last fling, in the hope of making them believe that it still has a right to hang around. If over the next 24 hours there should be any further disturbance, they (the person whose house it is) should say, simply and calmly, 'You know you have no right to be here now; you are to go as you have been directed.' When the spirit sees that they believe that it has nothing to hook on to, so to speak, it will have to leave. Such a 'last fling' does not often happen but, in case it should, I have found it is helpful to explain this, as it may avoid me having to make another visit.

Lesser and greater exorcism

In their book *Deliverance*, the Christian Deliverance Study Group speak of three forms of action available to those who minister in the realm of the occult: blessing, lesser exorcism and greater exorcism. The first, which may be accompanied by sprinkling with holy water, is simply a call to bring the power and love of God into a situation or upon a place. The main difference between the two forms of exorcism is that the lesser is in the form of a prayer to God, asking him to act to bring liberation, whereas a greater exorcism is a direct command to the evil forces that they should depart in the name of Christ. The Group stress that the latter should be used very rarely, and always with the express knowledge and permission of the exorcist's church authorities (for Anglicans, that is the bishop).

It will be recognised immediately that this conflicts with the suggested procedure I have set out above. I hesitate to disagree with the recommendations of the Group, and their warnings have caused me to question my own methods of ministry carefully. However, I am reluctant to abandon my own practice, developed over almost 30 years. I can say only that in dealing with the cleansing of places (and I must stress that, because deliverance of people is far more complicated and carries greater dangers), I have found it helpful to make a direct command to the evil entity to depart. Sometimes as I have done this, I have been very aware of the presence of evil, which can be frightening, and occasionally there has been a violent response as the thing goes, in the form of doors slamming and windows rattling. However, neither I nor the people present at the time have ever been attacked or suffered personal hurt or injury.

I believe that the main difference between the Group's view and my own is that they differentiate between the forms of procedure to be used, whereas I make the greater distinction between the infestation of places and of people. I find the Group's approach unnecessarily increases the tension by defining my normal procedure in respect of places as a 'greater exorcism' and thus importing (and possibly even imparting, at least in the mind of myself as the minister) to spirits a greater power than they have. My (possibly subconscious) approach has always been to regard these spirits, however evil they may be in themselves, as disobedient and annoying entities which have to yield in the name of the Lord Jesus Christ, because they know who he is and recognise his authority. With regard to the infestation of people, the problem, and therefore the danger, is far greater because there is often something within the mind, emotion or the will of the person who is suffering which allows the spirit to 'hook in', and this has to be dealt with before it can be dislodged. An additional consideration is that, in my experience, the spirits which seek to indwell people are greater and more powerful than those which infest places. On the whole, but certainly not always, the latter are mischievous and a nuisance rather than a danger. But more of that later.

Another area where I differ from the Group is in the matter of the source of the power which the spirits use. I have already raised the question of whether they are able in some way to tap into the electricity supply, because so often lights, clocks or other electrical equipment behave in an unusual fashion. The Group state that in their experience poltergeist phenomena are invariably associated with emotional stress between the people experiencing them. We cannot understand how this stress is transformed into the physical energy which the spirits can then use, but obviously some form of physical power is involved when objects are moved about or sounds produced, and this explanation, which the Group offer only as speculation, seems feasible, and I find it helpful. If I understand them aright, they would go further and hold that there is not necessarily any independent spirit, but somehow it is an outward expression of the disturbance within the personality (or personalities) involved.

In the light of this, the Group recommend, very reasonably, that the way to deal with the situation is to seek to relieve the stress, because this will result in the cessation of the activity. I do not question that, and undoubtedly, as ministers of God, the more we can do to bring peace and harmony in every situation the better. However, I can only state from my own experience that I have found commanding the thing to go has proved effective. As I understand it, the difference between the two methods is that I address the spirit in the name of Christ, commanding it to depart, whereas the Group seek to cut off the source of power producing the manifestation by reducing the stress factor of the people involved. In many cases, their method is obviously better because the result is that not only will the occult manifestations cease, but there will be greater harmony in the home. However, in circumstances where the people involved are unable or unwilling to take measures to reduce the stress, the manifestations will continue, whereas, in my experience, commanding the spirit to leave is effective, even if the situation causing the stress remains. However, later, when I relate some experiences involving the deliverance of people, I will give details of one case where my approach had little effect and the Group's suggested explanation regarding stress was probably correct.

Shortly before writing this, I was called to a flat where a young married couple were experiencing strange events. While they were out of the home, a teddy bear, which resided on a chair in the bedroom, would be placed on the middle of the bed, together with some other object – perhaps a card, which it appeared to be reading. There were a number of other manifestations similar to cases I have already mentioned. The only reason I refer to this one is that the couple volunteered the information that they found they were frequently becoming irritated with each other for no reason at all, but this happened only when they were in the flat. If they went out for a walk together, as soon as they were outside the flat the irritation dissipated. I suggested to them that if, as seemed probable, there was some spirit causing the problems, then it might well be creating the emotional stress to provide the source of the energy it needed – although the manifestations usually occurred while they were out. Anyway, I ministered as I have suggested above. I telephoned them some time later, and they reported that all was now well.

I am sometimes asked whether this ministry is effective if the family involved have no Christian faith. There are two things to say. First, the fact that they have called me in is an indication that they believe that as a Christian priest I may well be able to help. So there is at least a minimal faith. The other is that God is more gracious than I am. At one time, rather like Jonah, I felt that he ought not to have such mercy on those who not only ignored him but deliberately indulged in practices which the Bible condemns. Fortunately, I did not allow my personal views to prevent me from at least giving him an opportunity to work, and I acted in accordance with the ministry I have explained. He took and continues to take that opportunity. I do what I can to commend Christ, and I always explain that I have no power in my own right; evil spirits are not subject to me but to him. Beyond that, however, it is up to the Lord what he does when I act in his name.

While on the subject of non-believers, a parishioner who had been involved with a cleansing I had conducted told me an interesting story. A colleague of hers, whom I will call Jean, was aware of an 'oppressive presence' in her flat and, on occasions, she actually saw what she described as a blue light. It wasn't confined to any particular area, but pervaded every room. Apparently, she had had a rather uneasy relationship with her mother-in-law, who had not approved of her marriage to her son. The mother-in-law had, in fact, died in the flat, and Jean linked her to the oppressive presence. One day, she mentioned all of this to the parishioner, who innocently remarked, 'You know what my vicar would do? He would simply tell the thing to go in the name of Jesus.'

Jean went home and did just that. In recounting the story later, she told my friend, 'When I told it (her) to go in the name of Jesus, I am sure that I heard a scream. Immediately, the whole atmosphere lightened and there has been no more problem since.'

I would make a number of comments about this. Although Jean had studied theology at college, she made no particular profession of belief in Jesus. I am reminded of a story in Scripture:

> Some Jews who went around driving out evil spirits tried to invoke the name of the Lord Jesus over those who were demon-possessed. They would say, 'In the name of Jesus, whom Paul preaches, I command you to come out.' Seven sons of Sceva, a Jewish chief priest, were doing this. (One day) the evil spirit answered them, 'Jesus I know, and I know about Paul, but who are you?' Then the man who had the evil spirit jumped on them and overpowered them all. He gave them such a beating that they ran out of the house naked and bleeding. (Acts 19:13–16)

That related to a case of deliverance of a demonised man rather than an 'oppressive presence' in a home; nevertheless, I would not advocate such a course of action in the case of a non-believer (although apparently the Jewish exorcists had enjoyed some success prior to this particular case). However, we have no monopoly over the name of Jesus, and I cannot, nor would I wish to, control what another individual chooses to do regarding that name.

It can be argued, of course, that the whole situation regarding Jean and her mother-in-law was psychological and that she was simply projecting her unresolved unhappy relationship into the sense of the oppressive presence. Her action in commanding it to go provided the resolution of the problem. In any case, even if it was some form of occult manifestation, from what I have explained already it will be readily understood that I do not believe that it was, in fact, the spirit of her mother-in-law, or any other human being, but rather some manifestation feeding on the stress of the strained relationship.

Problems following cleansing

Unfortunately, most people find the paranormal intriguing. The number of films and TV programmes devoted to this subject is proof of the interest it arouses. I have found that occasionally, while people *say* that they want to be free of whatever manifestations are occurring, underneath there is a reluctance to see the thing depart totally.

I remember being called to a home where, in addition to small things being moved from one area only to appear in another, footsteps could be heard crossing a room. This was so vivid that when several members of the family were sitting together they could all track just where the footsteps were and the direction they were taking. I ministered in the way I have described, and all was well. However, about two weeks later I was called back to be told that the manifestations had started again. I found myself saying with a certainty that surprised myself, that if the manifestations had ceased then something must have happened to bring them back. At first, no one admitted to this, and the mother of the family, who was the one who had first called me in, was adamant that they had done nothing. I was strangely unwilling to believe this, although normally I would accept such an assurance.

Eventually, her son, who was about 18, admitted that he was responsible. He said that he was intrigued by the footsteps and rather liked having them around. They harmed no one, and he had asked them to come back (I didn't pursue how he had actually done the 'asking'). His mother rounded on him in anger and frustration, but he would not give way. In the end, I intervened to explain that there was no point in my engaging in any ministry. If I prayed, the thing might well go, but it would immediately return if a member of the household wanted it back. As and when they could agree that they *did* want to be rid of it, they could contact me again. I left, leaving the mother and son still arguing heatedly, and never heard from them again.

This experience helped me on a later occasion. The vicar of a neighbouring parish asked if I would help him deal with manifestations which were occurring in the home of one of his parishioners. He had arranged that we would arrive at the house at about 2 pm, and suggested that I should call at his vicarage some 20 minutes beforehand so that he could brief me on the background. I did this, and we were just about to set off together when his telephone rang. It was the owner of the house, asking where we were. As it was barely 2 pm, and the house was only round the corner, my friend was a little annoyed because he had been careful to state an approximate time. He explained that we were just about to leave and would be there within a few minutes.

As we turned into the street, we saw a large 'outside broad-casts' TV van parked outside the house, and I began to smell a rat. Sure enough, when we entered we found the front room full of TV equipment and its crew. The producer was eager to film 'the exorcism' as quickly as possible, in the hope that it could be broadcast that evening from the studio, which was over 80 miles away. It was he who had encouraged the house owner to telephone to hurry us up. There was also a freelance photographer there, who was hoping to take pictures which he could sell to the national press.

I must admit that I was annoyed at the discourtesy of the parishioner in not enquiring beforehand whether the vicar and I had any objection to 'performing' before the camera. I have objections on several grounds, not only because in my experience such activity does not lend itself to public display, and inevitably attracts criticism because somehow the camera seems to distort the action, which appears more dramatic than it may be in reality, but also because of the necessity to ask probing questions which may involve the family in having to reveal details of their behaviour that are distasteful. They will probably be reluctant to admit to this in public and so may give me false information. In short, I find the presence of the media inhibiting.

However, my principal objection, although I did not state this at the time, was that I had the suspicion that the family were enjoying their notoriety. It could only be because they had 'boasted' of what they were convinced was to be an exorcism that the media were there; how else could they have known of it? I doubted whether the family were truly sincere in wanting the manifestations to cease. Much to the annoyance of the TV producer, I refused to do anything while the team were present and, with an ill grace, they packed up their equipment and left.

There was nothing in particular to distinguish the manifestations from countless others. There were strange noises, and small articles would be moved, sometimes as though they had been thrown across the room. I ministered in my normal manner, warning the family that they must totally renounce all occult activity. They listened to what I had to say but I didn't feel they were particularly interested. I wasn't surprised to read in the local paper two weeks later that the family had called on the services of a medium!

More serious cases

Before leaving the subject of paranormal manifestation in places, I ought to mention that very occasionally these take a more sinister form.

I was once called to a house on a large housing estate, in an area where many Romany families had been housed. Such people are often particularly open to occult activity, many of them having psychic ability (I hesitate to call it a 'gift' because usually it is anything but). Indeed, it is very common that those who offer to read the palms of hands at fairs and seaside towns are gypsies.

When I arrived, the woman in the house was very frightened. On a number of occasions she thought she had noticed strange incidents – bedclothes rumpled or on the floor – but had managed to convince herself of some normal explanation. However, that morning she had made the bed in her son's room after he had gone to school, and had shut the door on leaving. Shortly afterwards, she had occasion to return to the room, and found the bedclothes pulled back and an indentation on the pillow and the bed as though someone had been lying there. She was alone in the house and was certain that no one had entered the room. I ministered in the way I have already described.

Incidentally, this produced its humour also. I called back a week later (when the children were home from school) and knocked on the front door. There was a sound of scuffling and then the woman's voice yelling, 'Get out the way, you bl . . . little b . . .' and she opened the door to see me standing there wearing my dog-collar. She recovered herself rapidly and gave me a polite smile. 'Oh, it's you, vicar,' she said. I explained that I was passing and just called to ask how things were. 'Oh, lovely, vicar; no more problems at all.'

Sometimes articles are moved with such force that they are broken, or people are bruised by, maybe, a piece of soap flying through the air with some force, but in my experience such incidents are rare. Rather more frequently, people tell me that during the night they have felt the bedclothes being pulled from them. It is difficult to assess the veracity of this because bedclothes can fall off as we move in our sleep, and if we are suddenly awakened our wits are not at their best. However, on occasions, people who sleep alone tell me that they have been involved in a mild tug-of-war over a bedspread or eiderdown. They even claim that they have felt someone actually getting into bed with them. It is easy to dismiss this, perhaps unkindly, as 'wishful thinking', but the distress they show as they tell me of the experience reveals that it is horribly real to them. Fortunately, whether it is real or their imagination, prayer seems to deal with the problem.

Young children will often speak of actually seeing someone who comes to them at night. In these cases it is very difficult to know what to believe. With their vivid imagination, it frequently happens that they invent imaginary friends to whom they refer by name. Single or lonely children are more likely to do this. But others speak of an 'old woman in a strange costume' – usually old-fashioned dress – who stands at the end of their bed and speaks to them.

One of the most unusual cases I have met was a young couple who called me round to their house urgently one morning. They claimed to have experienced a number of inexplicable events over the weeks, culminating the previous night in the wife being pulled out of her bed and dragged along the landing by some unseen force; she had only prevented herself being pulled down the stairs by grabbing the banister. I would like to believe that it was all in her imagination; however, it was so real to them that they refused to spend another night in the house, but wanted prayer before they left. As I do not know where they went, I was unable to follow them up, and I heard no more of the house.

Holy communion and cleansing

There are some priests who believe it right to cleanse an infested place by holding a service of holy communion on the site. Normally I do not do this because I do not believe that we are dealing with the soul of a departed person and, in most cases, the people who ask for my help are not church members, and I prefer not to involve them in something they do not understand. However, on two or three occasions I have held a communion service in the house, although in my experience this has not proved to be more effective than commanding the presence to depart.

A neighbouring incumbent contacted me to ask if I would accompany him to a home where a particularly disturbing series of events had occurred. A family of husband and wife with two children, a boy aged ten and a girl of about four, had lived in the house for some seven or eight years. From the outset, they had experienced a number of strange events; furniture would be moved and a fridge and washing-machine would be pulled out into the middle of the kitchen. As these latter items were under a work surface in a fitted kitchen, it would be difficult to grasp them and would require considerable energy to pull them out.

Surprisingly, the family had been prepared to put up with all this, regarding it simply as an annoyance; although on one occasion they had called at the local spiritist church and asked for help from three people who happened to be there at the time. According to the husband and wife, the three listened to the description of what had been happening and then expressed the view that no serious harm was being caused and there was nothing that they could do about it. They did not even call at the home.

However, over the previous three weeks, more sinister manifestations had occurred. The wife had been tied to a chair by her husband's belt while he was out; electric flex had been pulled out of an appliance, exposing bare wires, while the other end was still attached to the plug inserted in a socket; string and flex had been found, sometimes in the form a noose, on the bed-head near the wife and under her pillow, and she had heard a voice saying, 'I will get you.' Finally, one night when the husband, who had to leave home early to get to work, had gone up to bed and the wife was downstairs talking with a friend, something like a long boot lace had tied itself round each wrist, binding her hands together. The friend had watched it happen tremendously quickly. The husband was called, and he was able to release one end of the lace, but the other was tied so tightly that he had to cut it. It was this attack which made the two of them, husband and wife, contact the vicar. He called at the house, questioned the couple carefully, prayed in each room and held a communion service, in which the whole family participated. However, the manifestations continued, and it was then that he asked me to go with him to the home.

I also questioned the family, and elicited further information. It transpired that just about every form of paranormal manifestation had occurred, with the exception of noise – the furniture was being moved without anyone hearing anything at all. Radios, hi-fis and TV sets were being turned on when no one was in the house, there was a 'cold spot' in a particular room, there were unpleasant smells with no traceable cause, and the family cat, although it was willing to enter all the rooms, had on two occasions jumped suddenly off the bed and attempted to climb up the wall in panic. On the day we called, while the wife was out, something had happened in their bedroom which she had left for us to see. The husband had just returned from work, and we all went upstairs to find that the bed had been moved diagonally across the room and a fairly large drawer full of clothes had been removed from a chest and turned upside down on the bed, while a photograph album had been moved from a table and left open alongside the drawer.

Further questioning elicited the information that the previous occupant of the house had lost her father, following which she and her mother had gone to the spiritist church in order to contact him, and from then on they had continued to attend there on a regular basis. The husband and wife had contacted the previous occupant, whose mother had also now died, and she had come to the house and 'spoken' to the spirits, saying that as they were *her* parents they should leave that house and come with her to where she now lived, but this had not happened. The wife volunteered the information that when the furniture in the living room was moved it was to a position similar to the way the previous occupant had arranged hers.

The couple stated firmly that they had had no dealings at all with the occult (after I had explained what that involved) but it was at that stage that they mentioned their approach to the spiritist church, which had come to nothing. Nevertheless, in order to close any possible access, I asked them to confess and repent of contacting the spiritists, which they were very willing to do. I visited each room, commanding the evil to depart in the name of Jesus Christ, and we left. I commented to my colleague that I was astonished at how calm the family were and was surprised that they had put up with the regular movement of furniture over so many years.

Two days later, the incumbent contacted me again to say that something else had occurred, and the couple were distraught. We called at the home that evening. The husband and children were there, but the wife was out shopping. He explained that that morning he had been woken by a scream from his wife. Shoelaces had been removed from their little girl's trainers and tied, one on each of his wife's wrists, and then joined together. As she was waking, lying on her back, she had stretched her hands either side of her head, causing the tied laces to pull across her throat. She had been terrified.

In all my ministry (with one possible exception, related to an elderly, confused and lonely man who had been recently bereaved and claimed that his dead wife was haunting the house) I had never known such occurrences to continue after the procedure I had followed in this case. I suggested that we hold a service of holy communion in the home (although I was aware that their vicar had already done this), because I really did not know what else to suggest. The husband suggested that he should go to fetch his wife, explaining that she was in the supermarket nearby only because she was too frightened to stay in the house. When she returned, she was distraught;

her calmness on the occasion of our previous visit had been a front to conceal her fear in front of the children. She kept asking, 'Why is it attacking only me?'

I questioned them again about the intensification of the paranormal activity some three weeks earlier. Had anything unusual or stressful happened in the home at that time? The wife then admitted that about then she had been told that she had developed a serious medical problem. However, that had been dealt with the day before (i.e. between our two visits) and the doctors were very hopeful that she would suffer no recurrence. I pointed out that it was very interesting that the paranormal activity had increased at around the very time she was under particular stress. She replied that she was not conscious of any stress, as the same medical problem had arisen several years before and had been dealt with on that occasion and she was confident, therefore, that it would be dealt with on this. I suggested, nevertheless, that something must have caused the annoying but comparatively benign activity of the past seven or eight years to intensify into such personal attacks on her and, even if she was not aware of any stress, in the absence of any other explanation, that could be the cause of why the attacks were concentrated upon her. She then mentioned that her husband's belt, which had been in his jeans, and with which she had been tied up on the previous occasion, had once more gone missing, and she was terrified that it might appear again, perhaps round her neck!

In view of this, I laid my hands upon her and prayed that as the Scriptures proclaim 'if the Son sets you free, you will be free indeed' (John 8:36), she would indeed be set free from all attack. We then held a very shortened service of holy communion, in which everyone, including the children, received the bread and the wine. Any concern I might have had about allowing them to participate when they understood so little of what we were doing, was more than countered by the fact that *God* knew what we were doing, and to leave the children out would simply make them feel that they had been excluded from whatever protection we were claiming for the family.

Although the attacks were concentrated upon the wife, I believe that the manifestation came under the heading of cleansing of places rather than deliverance of a person because they came from outside her and, what is more, they happened only when she was in the house; they did not follow her around elsewhere.

The incumbent called about a week later to enquire how they were, but they were out at the time. Later, they left a message on his answering machine to say that string, in the shape of a noose, had again appeared.

I am still very dissatisfied about this case, because there are so many unanswered questions. At the outset both the incumbent and I wondered whether the wife could be perpetrating the binding on herself. Sometimes people who wish to move to another house 'invent' paranormal activity in order to encourage the authorities to offer this. However, in this case no such request had been made. Indeed, because we had not been able to clear the home, and as the attacks centred upon the woman were becoming more vicious, we suggested that they should inform the police. They were not happy about this, claiming that because the manifestations were clearly paranormal there was nothing that the police would be able to do, and they would probably dismiss them both as being mentally disturbed. I assured them that most police had encountered such things before – indeed, occasionally they contact the church for help – but the couple were unwilling to proceed in that direction. My colleague suggested that the husband and wife should seek an appointment with their doctor, and offered to accompany them as their vicar, to explain what had been happening. The husband was very willing for this but the wife was reluctant.

Having met with the family and seen the acute distress of the wife, my own belief is that she was genuine and not consciously responsible for any of these manifestations. However, I have to admit that all the attacks on her personally happened when her husband was either not in the room with her or, if he was, when he was asleep. She *could* have tied herself up, possibly to attract his attention for some reason. Admittedly there was the occasion when a friend witnessed the event, but my colleague and I had no opportunity to follow that up. This case remains one of the very few unsolved mysteries I have encountered.

It's all humbug!

Occasionally, humorous situations arise. I well remember a letter from my bishop, enclosing one he had received, with his comment, 'I think this is your field; perhaps you would look into it.' The original had been written by hand and read:

> Dear Sir, I recently heard on the radio the Bishop of Canterbury say that someone had lost a coat, which had gone missing from a cupboard. He said a prayer and it came back. A dressing-gown, which was in my wardrobe, has gone missing, and I'd be glad if you would come and say a prayer to bring it back. S. E. Briggs.

There was nothing to say whether the writer was male or female, and I could not trace the name in the telephone directory. It happened to be a Saturday and I decided to call that morning. It was a bungalow and, as I approached, I saw an elderly and very tiny woman in the garden. I had the letter in my hand. 'Mrs Briggs?' I enquired.

'Yes,' she said.

'The bishop has passed your letter on to me and asked me to call.'

'You'd better come in,' she said. 'You'll have to come round the side way; it's easier.'

We went round and entered the kitchen, where a middle-aged man and woman were sitting at the table, drinking coffee. 'My son and his wife; they've come to visit,' she explained to me. 'The bishop couldn't come himself, so he sent this man instead,' she explained to them.

We passed through the kitchen, down the corridor, and she led me into her bedroom. Clergy have to be very careful about that sort of thing, but she was very elderly and I thought I would be safe for a minute or two at least, before her son and daughter-in-law came to investigate.

'Let me explain what's happened,' she said. 'The dressing-gown was in this wardrobe; it belonged to my husband. He died last year, in this very bed. Of course, he'd been ill for some time, but not that ill. He had difficulty with his breathing, and one day, when the doctor had come to visit him, he said he thought he should get him to hospital as soon as possible. The ambulance men brought in a special chair thing and tried to get him into it, but, as you see, there isn't much room. One of them was standing just where you are now, and the other came round this side . . .'

I have come across such people before, and I am sure you have. They start to tell you something and go into such detail that it leads them down all sorts of side tracks, which are completely irrelevant. I didn't want to be rude, but she had been going full steam for almost five minutes, and we still hadn't got to her husband's death, let alone the dressing-gown, so at a moment when she paused, very briefly, for breath, I jumped in and said, 'But what about the dressing-gown?'

She was obviously put out and rather hurt. 'I'm telling you,' she said. 'I thought you would be interested in hearing about his death.' I felt duly rebuked. 'But still, if you want to know about the dressing-gown . . . It was always kept in here,' she explained, going to the wardrobe and opening it. It was crammed full of clothes hanging up. 'All his other clothes are here – look.'

It was so full that I felt she might easily have missed it. 'Are you quite sure it isn't there?' I asked.

'Of course I'm sure,' she exclaimed. 'I've had everything out.'

'It couldn't have got taken anywhere else?' I enquired.

'No, of course not,' she replied, irritated by my questions. 'It's gone missing. And I tell you that the Bishop of Canterbury said a prayer and that coat came back, and I want you to do the same for his dressing-gown.' I was not going to bother to explain that it was an *arch*bishop at Canterbury; that would only make matters worse. Obviously, an archbishop would have more influence with the Almighty than a bishop, but in her case she had only a common or garden parish priest.

'Well, I'll leave you to do whatever it is you have to do, and say your prayer,' she said. 'I'll be in the kitchen.' And with that, she left me alone in the bedroom.

I really did not know what to do. It seemed to me that the dressing-gown had simply been mislaid. Maybe her husband had been wearing it when he was taken into hospital. As I have explained, in cases like this, when people think they have heard or seen 'ghoulies and ghosties and three-legged beasties and things that go bump in the night', I like to pray in the presence of the person involved. However, S. E. Briggs was not with me, and I wondered if there was any point in my praying on this occasion, but I came to the conclusion that there was; I would feel better when I got home if I knew that I had prayed. I brought the old lady before the Lord, asking him to be with her in her loneliness, and I prayed that if there was anything strange about the disappearance of the dressing-gown, he would restore it to her. That hardly took any time at all, but I felt I couldn't return to the kitchen too soon or Mrs Briggs would think she had been sold short. On the other hand, I did not want to linger too long, because that might encourage her to think that I found this a particularly intriguing case. I tried to judge what she might consider an appropriate period, and returned to the kitchen, where the three of them were gathered.

'Well, I've prayed about the dressing-gown,' I said. 'So I'll be off now.'

'Thank you very much,' she said. 'I'll only get in touch with you again if the dressing-gown doesn't come back!'

That stopped me in my tracks. Talk about simple faith! I felt I had to respond in some way. 'I cannot guarantee it will return,' I explained. 'And if it doesn't, I fear there is nothing else I can do.'

Bishops receive a large number of letters. One bishop's wife told me it averaged between 30 and 40 a day. Because of the very nature of his job, almost all of them are requesting the bishop to do something, asking his advice on a problem, or complaining about something or other; very few letters are encouraging. I thought my bishop would like to be cheered up, so I wrote a light-hearted report of my experience with S. E. Briggs, shared the story with my wife, and then forgot about it.

About six months later, I received another letter; this time it came to me direct and not via the bishop.

Dear Sir, you came to my home some time ago to pray that my husband's missing dressing-gown would return, which it did three days later. I would like you to call again to pray for a tin of humbugs which has disappeared. I bought three tins when I was on holiday at Butlins. I gave one to Mr Scott, my neighbour, because he does odd jobs for me now that my husband has died and I don't want him to think I am not grateful. I gave another tin to my daughter-in-law, who is kind to me, and I put the third tin in a drawer, but it is not there now. Will you come and pray, and if the tin returns I will donate £1 to the church collection. S. E. Briggs.

I went to see her and, as it was not a Saturday, she was alone. I was regaled with the story of her holiday, together with a description of the tin of humbugs. On my previous visit I had not personally examined the wardrobe, and so on this occasion I asked if I might see the drawer from which the tin had vanished. Like the wardrobe, it was crammed full with a variety of articles but, as she moved them about, I could see clearly that there were no humbugs. I decided this time not to allow her to escape the prayer and, as she was closing the drawer, I said, 'I will pray now,' and launched into it before she could object.

I could pray with genuine thanksgiving for the return of the dressing-gown, but I must admit I felt a little foolish when it came to asking the Lord to oversee the return of the tin of humbugs. However, if no sparrow falls to the ground without the Lord knowing, why should he not be concerned about humbugs? Not for themselves as humbugs, but because their return, like that of the dressing-gown, might assure the old lady of his reality and his concern for her personally.

However, the church collection never received the £1, and if the tin *had* returned, I feel sure S. E. Briggs would have remembered her promise.

On my return home I wrote to the bishop again, to provide a little light relief in a busy day. Apparently the letter went round his office, causing considerable amusement. He replied, saying, 'So it is all humbug after all. I wish you could find some way of publishing the story.'

So I have.

2

The Deliverance of People

Preliminary observations

There are some Christians who do not believe in the existence of the devil. They admit that Jesus spoke of him as a reality, but they say that our Lord was a person of his times when it was common to attribute to satanic influence behaviour which today we realise is caused by mental or psychological disorder. Of course, our greater understanding of both medicine and the functions of the brain is of tremendous benefit; nevertheless, Scripture makes a clear distinction between sickness and demonic influence.

Indeed, for myself, the manner in which the Bible records the reaction of evil spirits to Jesus (e.g. 'I know who you are – the Holy One of God' [Mark 1:24] and, 'Two demon-possessed men coming from the tombs met him . . . "What do you want with us, Son of God?" they shouted' [Matthew 8:28–29]) is of greater significance in establishing the deity of Jesus than his ability to work miracles; the latter reveals only that in his humanity our Lord was so completely open to his

Father that the Father was able to work unhindered through him, in the power of the Holy Spirit (see John 14:10 and 1 Corinthians 12:6). However, the reaction of the demons testifies to the fact that they, who are of the spirit realm, recognise Jesus to be in himself the Holy Son of God.

Having said that, however, and convinced as I am of the reality of both the devil and evil spirits, in my experience demonisation is comparatively rare, certainly in the West, and the problem is far more likely to be psychological or mental. In ministering to people, I always look for some medical, mental or psychological explanation of their distress before ministering deliverance. There can be real danger in attempting deliverance where there is no demon present.

The case of the spirit and the hamster

On one occasion, a member of our young people's group believed that a fellow member was troubled by some evil spirit and decided he would 'deliver' her. I knew that she had had a traumatic childhood, although he did not, and I am as sure as I can be that before he interfered there was no demonic infestation involved. However, by the time he had performed his 'deliverance' she was in a terrible state. She was completely unable to speak or communicate in any rational way. Of course the young people were frightened by what had happened and only then did they call for me.

This was one of the most difficult situations I have faced. On several occasions the spiritual forces have been more powerful, but I have been involved with the deliverance from the outset; in this case I did not know what had been going on. Fortunately there were one or two mature Christians with me, one of whom had the gift of spiritual discernment. To my surprise she told me that she believed that a spirit of autism was involved. I had never heard of such a spirit (although I am now prepared to believe that there can be a spirit of just about anything), but I commanded the 'spirit of autism' to leave the girl. Within a very short time she had recovered sufficiently to be taken home, and there was no further trouble.

There was an interesting consequence to all this. It so happened that in the home where I had ministered to the girl there lived a young teenager; he was a Christian but he had just had an argument with his parents. It was a typical parent/teenager clash, where they had told him he could not do something or other he had wanted to do and, although he had obeyed, he was in a state of mental rebellion against them. The evening after I had ministered to the girl, the mother of this teenager telephoned me in great distress to say that her son had suddenly behaved in an extraordinary manner. He was in the bathroom and she heard him making a strange noise. She called through the locked door, asking if he was all right. He was unable to answer her, but with some difficulty was eventually able to open the door. He then sat on the stairs, where he banged his head on the wall while making a strange grunting sound, which was remarkably similar to the behaviour the previous night of the girl who had apparently been under the influence of the 'spirit of autism'. His mother told him to stop, but he continued to do it for some time. In discussing the matter with him later, he told me that he had wanted to stop but could not do so. What he found even more frightening was that he couldn't move his jaw, and was therefore unable to explain the situation to her.

Fortunately, the mother was a mature Christian and had sensibly called on the name of Jesus for protection of her son. Having persuaded him to lie down on his bed, she had then telephoned me. By the time I arrived, he had recovered. Of course, I prayed with them both, but I believe her calling on the name of Jesus had been sufficient to set him free from whatever had attacked him. I am still in touch with him, over 25 years later, and there has been no recurrence of the problem.

Further investigation revealed that the family owned an elderly pet hamster, which had fallen sick the morning of the day on which the girl had been 'delivered'. In fact the hamster was dying, and it actually expired the following night – when the son of the house had behaved so strangely. Immediately after his recovery, his parents discovered that the hamster was dead. My theory of what had happened is that, when the over-eager young man had decided to practise deliverance on the young girl, some evil spirit had found an opportunity of gaining access to her because she was in some psychological distress, due to his insensitive and foolish actions. My minis-tering in the name of Jesus had indeed set her free but I had omitted to make the spirit subject to Jesus and, on leaving the girl, it had gone into the nearest unprotected living thing – the sick hamster. When this died, the spirit sought another haven, and finding the teenager who, at that moment, was vulnerable because of his rebellious attitude, entered him, but because he was a believer it was not able to gain any deep or lasting access, and the mother's action in calling on the name of Jesus was all that was needed to get rid of it.

Of course, I have no means of verifying this theory, but it does fit the facts. It seems too great a coincidence for the teen-ager to have manifested almost identical behaviour to that of the girl the night before, particularly as he had not been present to witness what had happened then. We know, also, from the story of the demoniac men and the Gadarene swine, that evil spirits hate to be disembodied and will seek somewhere to dwell. Some months later I had the opportunity to share my theory with Dom Robert Petitpierre. He agreed that my explanation was most probably correct.

Following this experience, I prefer not to minister deliverance if there are children or young people in the vicinity. Should it be totally unavoidable, which is only very rarely, I will do so because I do not believe we should be subject to the enemy's agenda; Jesus is greater than the powers of darkness. I will take care, however, to place everyone in the house under the protection of his name and to make every spirit subject to him.

Possession versus oppression

Some people differentiate between possession and oppression by evil spirits. While this can sometimes be useful, it is not scriptural. The Bible in its original language speaks simply of people being demonised, without stating to what degree they may be affected. However, John's Gospel records that when Judas took the sop, the devil actually entered him (John 13:27). We need to remember that the devil is seeking to do all the harm he can, and is particularly concentrating his attack on Christians (who are obviously a greater threat to him than unbelievers), without any direct occult involvement on our part. The latter simply affords him an opportunity for greater influence over us. We will look further at whether a Christian can be demonised in Chapter 3.

Distinguishing between mental disorder and demonisation

I am sometimes asked how we can know whether someone is suffering from demonic attack, or whether the problem is mental or psychological. It is not always easy to decide. Often it seems that there may be a combination of causes. Medics may treat the person with drugs and, when there is some definite improvement, they believe that this proves that the problem is totally one of mental disorder. On the other hand, I have met with some Christian ministers who seem prepared to exorcise anything that moves; they minister deliverance and they, also, see some improvement and so they assume that the problem is totally spiritual. In fact, in some cases it may well be that both the drugs and the spiritual ministry have contributed their particular benefits. Human beings are a whole – body, soul and spirit – and each area affects the other two. It is hardly surprising that Satan and his minions, seeking to disrupt God's creation, should do all they can to cause physical and mental illness in those to whom they have gained some access. Similarly, I am open to the view that in particular cases (certainly not all) where there is sickness it may be that a person's spiritual defences are down or weakened, allowing the possibility of some degree of access for evil spirits.

How evil spirits gain access to individuals

It is my understanding that human beings are born with a protective spiritual 'shield' but this can (although not necessarily will) be breached in a number of ways:

- involvement in Satanism, witchcraft or black magic;
- involvement in spiritism (contacting spirits through seances, the Ouija board, glass moving, etc.);
- involvement in other occult activities, such as reading tarot cards, etc.;
- abortion;

- deliberate sin, especially pornography and sexual perversion;
- severe traumatic experience, causing extreme fear, shock or panic (see below).

Also, my own experience of dealing with various cases has led me to the belief (although I cannot recall seeing this written elsewhere) that the act of sexual intercourse with someone who is already demonised can allow spirits to pass from one person to another. I have also discovered that spirits which are within women who are pregnant are able to pass to the unborn foetus. Indeed, I would go so far as to say that it is my experience that those who are practising spiritist mediums invariably have children who are born with spirits already within them.

Two cases of traumatic experience

A man in his fifties manifested symptoms which were similar to demonisation and, when he came to ask me about the possibility of deliverance, I questioned him extensively about his childhood. Among other things, he told me of an occasion when he hid in terror under the table while his parents, having a violent quarrel, threw plates, forks and even knives at each other. As he described the incident, it was as though he was reliving the experience. Because of his own doubts, I did minister deliverance very gently, but there was no obvious reaction. I believe that this was a case requiring counselling, which I gave, and that no evil spirit was involved.

On another occasion, however, a young woman asked to see me on the advice of her friends, who were concerned about her. She had been a Christian for some time, but had recently joined a church where she learned for the first time about being filled with the Holy Spirit and exercising his gifts. The evening before coming to see me she had been at a homegroup and, in the course of this, she had a word of knowledge, or a prophecy, which she became more and more convinced was for another member sitting across the room. However, she was far too shy and timid to share it. As the meeting progressed, she became more and more agitated because of the pressure on the one hand to be obedient to what she believed the Lord was asking her to do and, on the other, her fear of making a fool of herself. Eventually, her desire to be obedient to her Lord carried the day and, in front of the others, she crossed the room and, standing in front of the person she believed the message was for, spoke it out. I gather that the word was indeed relevant and meaningful to the person involved, but it was the consequence of her action that caused her friends such concern. Suddenly she reacted with unnatural movements and, at the same time, spoke in a strange and very unpleasant unrecognisable language, which her friends believed was demonic and certainly not a manifestation of the Holy Spirit. It was this which made them suggest she should come to ask if I could give any advice.

I asked her if there had been any further strange manifestations and she said there had not; in fact, she had felt particularly at peace, with a greater sense of the Lord's presence than she could ever recall and, but for the insistence of her friends, she would not have bothered to come to me. At the time, although I had had some training in how to deal with the occult, I was not very experienced in practice. I can say only that, as I listened to her, I found myself asking unusual questions. I have since come to recognise this as the guidance of the Spirit. The experience is difficult to describe. I do not hear any words; I can say only that I just 'know' what to do. I am aware that this may appear to be big-headed or boastful, but that is not my intention; indeed, properly understood, I believe that it is a form of receptive humility; it is simply believing that Jesus spoke the truth when he said that the Holy Spirit would lead us into all truth. Certainly I am claiming no skill or ability for myself; I am seeking simply to be open to the Lord and what he is doing. In the case of this young woman, I found myself asking her if she could ever recall an experience of extreme fear or terror when young. Without hesitation, she told me the following story.

When she was a very little girl, so her mother had told her much later, she had been very difficult at bedtime. Her parents would settle her in bed but, most nights, she would come downstairs after half an hour or so. Very unwisely, her father, in an attempt to put a stop to this, told her that the Sandman came round every night, looking for little girls who would not stay in bed. The Sandman would come to the window and, if he saw any little girl who was still awake, he would tap on the window and demand to take her away for ever and ever. One evening, when she had once again come downstairs, her uncle had called at the house. Assuming his young niece was safely asleep, rather than ring the bell, which he thought might wake her, he had tapped on the window to attract attention. The little girl was so terrified that, in order to reach her mother, who was in the kitchen, she clambered onto a chair and then onto the table to reach the serving hatch into the kitchen. Her mother told her that although the base of the hatch was made of formica, in her terror the little girl had actually scratched the surface with her nails. I still find it difficult to understand how that could be, but there is no doubt it was a traumatic experience for that little girl. As she finished her story, I 'knew' what had happened. At that moment of extreme terror, a spirit of fear had gained access to the little girl and, without being able to dominate her totally, had caused her to be a somewhat fearful person, unsure of herself all her life from then on. Her decision to overcome her fear in obedience to Jesus finally deprived the spirit of its hold upon her. In Scripture, we hear of spirits leaving people with screams; in the case of this young woman, apparently it used a demonic tongue. I felt confident in advising her that because of her obedience to what she believed the Lord wanted of her (and remember that the first sin of mankind was *dis*obedience), the spirit's power to trouble her was broken and the Lord had set her free. I suggested that she need not fear a repeat of the unpleasant experience of the night before. That was well over 20 years ago and there has been no recurrence of the problem.

Note: One of the gifts of the Spirit is the ability to 'speak in other tongues'. This simply means in a language that is not consciously known to the speaker; it may be a human language or a heavenly or angelic one (1 Corinthians 13:1). According to Scripture, it is always addressed by mankind to God (1 Corinthians 14:2) and not by God to mankind. (See also 1 Corinthians 14:14, 16 and 17, where the speaker is described as praying, praising or giving thanks – i.e. speaking to God, not receiving messages from him.) This is frequently misunderstood and many charismatic fellowships believe that God will sometimes convey a message from himself in a tongue which has to be interpreted by someone who has the gift of interpretation (also a gift of the Spirit). I believe that such an 'interpretation' is, in fact, a prophecy or a word of knowledge (yet other gifts of the same Holy Spirit) and the original 'tongue' remains uninterpreted; a correct interpretation of it would be in the form of praise, thanksgiving, intercession or petition addressed to God. Personally, I have enough difficulty in hearing and understanding God when he speaks to me in my native tongue, without him confusing me even more by speaking in a language which requires interpretation. On the other hand, when it comes to me speaking to him, I rapidly run out of words to convey my love and praise. It is a great relief not to have to search for words, but to allow the Holy Spirit to inspire my own spirit to pour out my feelings freely in a language he gives. Satan seeks to ape this gift, but the tongues or languages he supplies to his followers are very harsh and unpleasant, and it requires little spiritual discernment to recognise their source.

3

Deliverance From What?

At this stage, it might be sensible for me to make three comments. First, the ministry of deliverance is not an exact or even quantifiable science. It cannot be measured, any more than can the effectiveness of prayer. All that can be said about the effectiveness of prayer is: 'I prayed and such and such happened.' There is no scientific proof of the link between the prayer and the event. Similarly with deliverance; some may be convinced that an evil spirit must have been involved, while others may believe that the problem was psychological, and the ministry simply triggered a psychological release. Spiritual truths are not understood by the mind alone. In the words of Paul to the Corinthians: 'The man without the Spirit does not accept the things that come from the Spirit of God, for they are foolishness to him, and he cannot understand them, because they are spiritually discerned' (1 Corinthians 2:14).

Second, while a few general principles can be laid down explaining methods of dealing with deliverance – and I will share later such as I know – most information will be gained by experience, which is why it is helpful to adopt the method employed by Jesus in training his disciples; first, they watched him minister, then he watched them minister and finally he sent them out in twos to minister in his name. This is why so much of what I share here is anecdotal.

Finally (and I am aware of the frustration I will provoke by saying this), while we all desire to have set procedures to follow, and the experience of what 'worked' on previous occasions is often useful background information, if you are called to this ministry you will 'know' at the time what to do. Perhaps it is similar to the instruction Jesus gave to his disciples about not worrying in advance what to say to their accusers when they were brought to trial: 'Do not worry about how you will defend yourselves or what you will say, for the Holy Spirit will teach you at that time what you should say' (Luke 12:11–12). Ministering deliverance is to operate in the realm of faith and, as John Wimber used to say, 'Faith is spelt R-I-S-K.'

I have mentioned in the introduction that almost 30 years ago my bishop sent me on a residential training course run by the Bishop of Exeter's Commission on Exorcism. The chairman, Dom Robert Petitpierre, shared with us a number of his experiences, which held us enthralled, until he reached the climax, when we expected him to tell us how he ministered in each case. He invariably passed over this with the phrase, 'So I did the necessary and all was well.' Together with everyone else on the course, I became totally frustrated until eventually we asked, 'But what *was* the necessary? What did you *do*?' He looked at us as though taken by surprise. 'You will know at the time what to do,' he said. 'You will know at the time.' I find it rather amusing that all these years later I find myself saying exactly the same thing.

The use of psychic abilities

Dom Robert was psychic. In his case, it enabled him to 'see' spirits. I deliberately do not describe this as a psychic 'gift' because usually it is anything but a gift. He told us that his brother had the same ability. On one occasion, when they were staying in an old and somewhat stately home, on passing through the hall into one of the rooms, he noticed a man in old-fashioned dress sitting on a chair by the door. His brother, following him into the room, asked, 'Did you see him?' 'I did,' replied Dom Robert.

I gather that while they were able to 'see' such spirits, there was something different about them (the spirits) which allowed the brothers to recognise that these were not ordinary human beings. It might be thought that this ability would be useful in assessing the situation, and deciding what action was needed when dealing with the occult. However, Dom Robert insisted that whenever he had tried to use his psychic ability in cases of deliverance, it had always caused more problems than it solved because it conflicted with the guidance and ministry of the Holy Spirit. Over the years, he had worked to suppress it, mainly by refusing to use it, and by the time I knew him the 'ability' had just about left him.

Watchman Nee, a great Christian pastor and teacher in the first half of the twentieth century, in his book, *The Latent Power of the Soul* (Christian Fellowship Publishers), tells how he had discovered that he had the ability to ascertain people's thoughts after only a brief conversation with them, in a sort of telepathic way. As a young Christian, he thought that this ability was very helpful in his work for the Lord. But as he became more experienced he dared not used it, and resisted it with prayer.

Perhaps I should refer here to other forms of ESP, such as dowsing (holding a twig or rod under tension and walking across an area until it twists, thus indicating the presence of water or metal, etc.). I really cannot speak with authority on the subject, for I have had virtually no experience of it, nor do I understand it. For myself, I am attracted by the explanation that in the time of mankind's innocence we had many gifts which are not generally manifested today. Perhaps telepathy and dowsing are the remnants of two of them.

In view of the vast range of responsibilities laid upon mankind in the opening two chapters of Genesis (to subdue the earth, as Jesus subdued the storm, and to have dominion over the animals) it would not be surprising if God had initially given such gifts which fell into abeyance, or which he deliberately rendered inoperative, following our disobedience at the Fall. At present, I am agnostic with regard to such abilities. I am uneasy about their use, but I feel I have no specific grounds to condemn them.

I understand that some, if not all, of the members of the Christian Deliverance Study Group are open to the use of what they may regard as 'natural' gifts of psychic power or ability. Personally, I side with Dom Robert and Watchman Nee on this and believe that it is better to allow such powers to fall into abeyance and rely only on the guidance of the Holy Spirit.

I would add in this respect that there is one aspect of the healing ministry which has always concerned me – the use of what Watchman Nee calls the latent power of the soul, to which I have referred above. When first I entered upon the healing ministry generally (as opposed to the specifically deliverance aspect) I was sometimes tempted to 'will' the person to be well. I imagined that there was some energy within myself, albeit given by God, which I could release upon or into the person for whom I was praying.

I was intrigued by the experience of our Lord Jesus who, when the woman with the issue of blood touched his garment and was healed, felt power go out of him (Luke 8:46), and also the comment of Peter to the cripple at the beautiful gate that he had no silver or gold but he did have something he could give (Acts 3:6) and then ordered the man to be healed, as though he had that power within him as a personal possession to be used. However, in fact I never did try to project any such personal power upon anyone, because I felt a check in my spirit. Now, when I minister healing I picture myself as an empty vessel, a channel through whom the Holy Spirit can flow. I am simply 'earthing' or incarnating the presence of Christ. I am exerting no personal power at all. This attitude is, I believe, even more important in the field of the deliverance ministry. I am careful not to take any power or authority to myself. Like an ambassador, the authority I have, and I *do* have authority, is that bestowed by Jesus. It cannot be stored, but is a living, dynamic force flowing directly from him and is active only while I abide in him.

Extrasensory Perception (ESP)

From time to time I have met up with people who have different forms of ESP, and it usually causes distress. A common form is for a person to know in advance that some disaster is about to happen. Most of us have heard of cases where someone has had an overwhelming impression that he or she should not travel on a particular plane and has cancelled the flight, only to discover later that it has been involved in some accident. It is difficult to claim that such a premonition is evil;

after all, in Scripture, God often warned people through dreams. I have in mind, rather, occasions when someone has a premonition of some international disaster, such as an earthquake, the sinking of a ship or a major train accident, and they experience the distress of 'seeing' the victims suffer. There is nothing they can do to prevent the event – usually they have no idea where or when it will happen – but, when it does, they have a feeling of guilt that somehow, because they had the warning, they bear some responsibility. I have no idea why these people have this ability, and personally I have never found anyone who has actively sought it. (There is a tradition that the seventh child of a seventh child is psychic but I have never, so far as I know, met up with such a person, and so I am unable to confirm this.) In Acts 16:16–18 we are told of a slave girl who had a spirit of divination by which she predicted the future. In that case, Paul ministered deliverance. I am not convinced that the cases I personally have met have required the casting out of a spirit, but I do believe that the ability is of the occult and not of God. I usually ask the person to renounce the ability and then I minister in the name of Jesus, shutting the door to their spirit and mind which has allowed the powers of darkness access to trouble them in this way. I may also make the sign of the cross on their head. In my own limited experience, this has been sufficient to set them free.

Electronic Voice Phenomenon (EVP)

In recent years, there has arisen an interest in what is termed EVP. This involves the use of a microphone and tape recorder. Both are activated, and the operator either leaves it alone or may speak out in a similar manner to a spiritist medium, or a person using a Ouija board, inviting a spirit or a 'dead' person to step forward and leave a message. Except on very rare occasions, nothing is heard through their physical hearing but, when the tape is rewound and played, a voice is heard speaking. It is usually indistinct and distorted – rather similar to the voice of the Daleks in the BBC programme *Dr Who*.

Participants claim to recognise the voice or the laugh of some relative who has died. As with the case of seances, the messages are very bland and uninteresting, but are able to convince those who receive them that it is the person they purport to be, and thus provide evidence of life after death.

However, as we have seen, the Bible speaks of familiar spirits, and it seems that these are very aware of facts and events in the life of the individual they impersonate. When they refer to these, the relatives who listen to them assume that it must, indeed, be their loved one who is speaking, for who else could possess such detailed information?

It seems that EVP began about 50 years ago, i.e. when tape recording became available to the general public. With the easy access to cassette tape recorders at low cost, the interest in EVP has developed over the past 20 years or so. Channel 4 broadcast a programme on the subject in December 2001, in the course of which it was reported that Pope Pius XII showed great interest in the phenomenon, and declared that it was not similar to spiritism. In my opinion, the two are identical; both are attempts to contact the dead, which, as I have shown, is expressly forbidden in Scripture. I have no idea how it occurs, but neither have those who are persuaded that it is genuine. If the spirits are able to use some form of energy, which they take from those who play with the Ouija board, it seems to me very likely that they are able to tap into the electrical power used to work the tape recorder. I have already mentioned that one of the manifestations in the case of paranormal occurrences in places is that electrical equipment behaves erratically.

I must admit that I have never yet come across anyone who has admitted to being involved in EVP, probably because it is not nearly as widespread as working the Ouija board, but I believe it to be dangerous and something to be avoided.

Alternative medicine

I am aware that some Christians who specialise in the healing ministry, including deliverance, refuse to minister in any way to people who have been involved in dowsing, telepathy, hypnotherapy and any form of ESP unless they have first renounced and repented of all such involvement, claiming that these are all of the occult. They also demand the same in respect of involvement with most forms of alternative medicine, including acupuncture and homeopathy. There are some who hold that there are spiritual dangers associated with being anaesthetised for an operation, because an evil spirit may enter while the person is unconscious. I must be careful what I say here, because I would not want to be responsible for encouraging anyone to experiment in areas which may cause distress or even harm to their spiritual well-being. I will share my own views, but I must stress that they are no more authoritative than those of anyone else.

I believe very strongly that there are areas of activity which are clearly of the occult and, as such, are forbidden to us. One obvious illustration is the practice of 'magic', white as well as black. (I will give an example of this later.) In the area of alternative medicine, there are some practitioners who make their diagnosis by means of tarot cards, or by holding a pendulum over an area of the patient's body and reading meaning into the type of 'swing' this produces. For me, such methods are not simply strange; I believe they are dangerous. However, I believe it to be arrogant to assume that it is only we in the West who have discovered effective means of treatment and developed medical skills, and surely it is foolish to dismiss the learning of other ancient cultures.

Acupuncture

This is an ancient art or skill, which was developed by the Chinese at least 2,000 years ago, and possibly more. One report I have read claims it was discovered by chance in the course of a war. It was noticed that some warriors wounded by arrows were healed of a number of complaints from which they had been suffering previously. This led to the recognition of certain pressure points in different parts of the body, which led, in turn, to the development of the art of acupuncture. As any culture would do, the Chinese assimilated this new knowledge into their beliefs and developed the theory of the yin and the yang as the balancing life forces flowing through the human body, which can be controlled by inserting needles into the various pressure points. It seems to me that whether these pressure points exist or not is simply a matter of fact, without it being necessary to adopt the theory of the yin and the yang. Acupuncture has proved successful in treating certain sicknesses in animals, as well as human beings, and I am not convinced by those who state with such assurance that it is, of itself, of the occult and dangerous, when they are simply stating opinions without giving any clear reasons for them.

Homeopathy

With regard to homeopathy, I can speak with a little more authority. My wife suffered from psoriasis which, over a period, developed until it covered the whole of her arms and legs. It was both extremely uncomfortable and unsightly. She was referred to a hospital consultant, who admitted that Western medicine could do little for her, but suggested that she should try a new steroid cream on a particular area of her ankle, to see if it helped. Not only was it of no benefit, but it damaged the skin so badly that it left a permanent weakness and an ugly stain. A Christian friend recommended that she consult a particular homeopath, who was also a registered GP. This doctor warned her that it might take him more than one attempt to discover the correct treatment and, indeed, his first two attempts were not successful, but within three weeks he had found the right prescription, which cleared the psoriasis completely within a matter of days.

I have tried to discover just what objections some Christians have to homeopathy, and I have been given a variety of explanations. The first is the method of diagnosis. I have already stated that I will have nothing to do with those who swing pendulums, etc., but the homeopath specialist who treated my wife simply asked detailed questions. His argument (and that of other reliable practitioners) was that he was treating the person and not the sickness; that is to say, 'straight' medical practice prescribes a medicine to attack and defeat a particular disease, irrespective of who happens to be suffering from it, but homeopathy is based on the belief that different people may require different treatment for the same illness, because the intention is to build up that person's own immune system. This seems to me to be certainly as acceptable as the Western method, and perhaps better.

The second objection is that the substance used in the medication has been diluted so drastically and so many times that nothing of it can be chemically traced by the time the final dilution is administered; therefore, the argument goes, it must be of the occult. But it is a dangerously irrational form of argument to say that if something is not 'a' it must be 'b', when no one is able to say what or how many alternatives there may be. For myself, I expect that science will one day discover a new area of natural activity which will explain how and why homeopathy works. Already there has been considerable work done in bio-energetic research, although I am not qualified to suggest that the explanation will, in fact, lie in that area.

A third objection is that the medicines are prepared according to all sorts of strange rituals (e.g. left overnight in the light of the full moon). I find it difficult to believe that Nelson's, a major manufacturer in England of homeopathic medicines, can work on this principle, bearing in mind the vast number of medicines involved.

The fourth objection is that Samuel Hahnemann, who first discovered and developed homeopathy, was a Freemason and therefore, so the argument goes, may well have been influenced by the occult. But two plus two equals four, whatever the character and beliefs of the person who discovered it. Either it is truth or it is not.

Finally, and this is perhaps the most serious objection, those who use homeopathy are hindered in their spiritual progress. Again, I can speak only from my own experience, which is that some of the Christians I have most admired and who have taught me most, have happily used homeopathy. My wife continued to grow closer and closer to the Lord before she died from a congenital heart condition. It would have been grossly unfair to have prevented her from obtaining the relief she did from psoriasis, a terrible complaint, because of what I believe is the unsubstantiated prejudice of some Christians whom, in other respects, I hold in great regard.

I do believe that we need to approach all forms of alternative medicine with care, to ensure that they are not based on false spiritual principles. Indeed, personally I have reservations about hypnotherapy, because here an individual's control of him or herself is taken over by another person, and I wonder whether an evil spirit may also be able to take the opportunity to gain access in some way while the 'door is open'. This, of course, is totally different from anaesthesia, where there is no intention to manipulate the mind, or control or influence another person's behaviour. I do not have sufficient experience in this area to come to an informed conclusion.

I fear that some Christian leaders, in expressing their views on alternative medicine, have been guilty of throwing the baby out with the bath-water, through ignorance or prejudice, and they communicate their views to members of their flock, who then adopt them simply because they respect these leaders, but without being able to give any logical reason for their belief.

Freemasonry

The majority of colleagues whom I know personally and who are involved in the ministry of deliverance are convinced that there is a 'spirit of Freemasonry', which needs to be cast out of those who practise the craft. I must be honest and say that I have never had to do this, but it may be simply fortuitous that I happen never to have met a case which required it. I am very concerned that for some people Freemasonry is a substitute religion and, certainly, I know devout and deeply committed ministers who have told me that they have experienced deep-rooted opposition from their congregations where several of the members are Freemasons. These congregations have a form of Christianity in that they profess orthodox doctrine, but in practice they deny the *power* of it. Colleagues tell me that they have never known a practising Freemason who demonstrated any of the gifts of the Holy Spirit, and neither have I, but, as I have already stated, arguments based on negative statements are not conclusive. I can say only that if and when I meet up with a person where there is a possibility of demonisation, and who is or has been involved in Freemasonry, I will share my concerns and will investigate the possibility that a spirit may be involved.

Multiple Personality Disorder

As with the cleansing of places, it is helpful to try to establish what gave rise to the person being demonised. I am always reluctant to believe that it is a matter of demonisation if there is no reason for it. Some people may believe themselves to be demonised when they are not – they require counselling, and may exhibit symptoms which appear to be demonisation yet are something else. There are some psychiatrists, particularly in the USA, who believe that there is a condition called Multiple Personality Disorder (MPD). As far as I understand this, it may develop because the person had some traumatic experiences when young. These are so distressing that the child develops a defence mechanism by pretending that these things are not happening to him or her but to another person, whom they invent in their imagination, even giving this other person a name. The good things in life happen to him or her (the real person). The nasty things happen to George or Brenda – that is, the person of the imagination. Finding some relief in this, they may invent other such characters. The problem arises when they live out these different personalities, sometimes claiming, 'George told me to do that.' It is easy to understand how such a condition can appear to be demonic infestation by an evil spirit. In fact, it is, as the term describes, a multiple personality disorder, requiring not deliverance but very careful counselling to integrate the various personalities into the one personality that the person is.

I must make clear that by no means all psychiatrists accept that there is such a condition as MPD, and they would give other explanations for such behaviour. It is beyond my competence to say anything further on this matter.

Stored pain

Another condition which may be confused with deliverance is stored pain. Sometimes people have had to endure much hurt over many years, and have been unable to express it. It may begin in childhood, and maybe they were beaten if they cried or if they complained, or perhaps they resorted to denial in order to make their lives bearable. When the truth dawns on them that God really does love them and they respond to him, the Holy Spirit may open the door to the 'spiritual room' within them where they have stored the pain and, in the release, they may produce a long and high-pitched wailing. It is easy to assume that it is a demon reacting to the person opening up to God. But it is probably not demonic at all.

Can a Christian have an evil spirit?

Another matter I should address is whether a Christian can be demonised. Opinions differ: some would hold that this is impossible. 'How can an evil spirit dwell in a person who belongs to Jesus?' they argue. I have discovered that those who hold this view are so convinced that it must be correct that if it is later shown that a professing Christian has indeed been delivered of an evil spirit then, in order to preserve their theory, they will claim that it was not a genuine profession; only after deliverance can such a person truly accept the Lord.

For myself, I would agree that once a person has become a Christian, he or she cannot become demonised while they are holding to Christ. However, if an evil spirit is already indwelling them when they become a believer, it may well not relinquish its hold without a struggle or, alternatively, it may seek to conceal its presence. In past ages, the Christian church ministered a mild form of exorcism at the time of baptism. The vestiges of this custom remain in our baptism service today, though not as clearly as in the past. For instance, in many liturgies, at the time of the baptism, the priest says something along the lines of: 'May Almighty God deliver you from the powers of darkness, and lead you in the light and obedience of Christ.'

I have known a number of sincere Christians who were suffering some form of spiritual oppression who, after deliverance, experienced a new freedom. However, I believe it would be totally irresponsible to claim that they were not really seeking to follow Christ before the deliverance had taken place. I believe that anyone who confesses Jesus Christ as Lord and seeks to follow him belongs to him.

If a person is demonised, it is advisable to deliver them of the demon before praying for them to be filled with the Holy Spirit. Otherwise the battle between the Spirit and the demon may take place inside them, which can be unnecessarily disturbing.

Different forms of occult oppression

As with the cleansing of places, there can be a number of different forms of occult oppression of people. One of the most unusual – indeed the only one of its type which I have encountered – was referred to me by a friend of a friend.

A married woman in her thirties explained that she had a son (I will call him John), an only child, who was aged about six and at a private prep school. The headmaster had asked to see her and her husband. He told them that he was concerned because their son was behaving in a peculiar manner, which he had never met in any other child. It was almost as though he had a split personality, one moment behaving in one way, and the next in another. Neither was particularly bad nor by itself would attract comment; it was the inconsistency which disturbed him. Also, he and his staff had noticed that the lad frequently spoke to himself, yet as though he were addressing another person. His mother had not noticed this behaviour at home but, following the headmaster's comments, and being alerted to it, she had indeed become aware of some rather strange behaviour. She asked whether I thought he could be under attack from some spirit.

Although the mother had said that her boy was an only child, I thought it right to ask her if she had ever had any other children. She was doing her best to be completely open and, after only a brief hesitation, she admitted that she had become pregnant before her marriage by the man who was now her husband. They had both agreed that she should have an abortion. Although I did not seek further details, she volunteered the information that the aborted foetus was a boy.

I had not had very much experience of the occult at that time, and had not learned that my 'hunches' were very often the leading of the Spirit. However, I shared with her the possibility that the aborted child, having been deprived of life and not having had any funeral service commending his soul to God, was seeking to live out his life through the body of his full brother. (I use the term 'full brother' because both children shared the same parents.)

I had had the benefit of listening to Dr Ken McCall, who is a qualified doctor and psychiatrist, and who had been a medical missionary. As I have already explained, he was one of the original members of the Bishop of Exeter's Commission. He has done a great deal of work investigating ancestry, and has since written a book called *Healing the Family Tree* (Sheldon Press). I am not sure that I can go along with all he says, or can agree that his theories are applicable in as many cases as he suggests; however, he opened my eyes to a whole area of occult oppression of which I was entirely ignorant. I am also grateful for his suggestions on how this can be overcome.

I proposed to the mother that we should hold 'a communion service with intent'. (I expect my colleagues with a High-Church background would call it a requiem, although of an unusual kind.) I asked if her husband would like to be present, but she gave me the impression that, while he was willing for her to continue her own investigations into the possible spiritual cause of their son's behaviour, he did not wish to be involved. So it was agreed that the mother, together with the mutual friend who had accompanied her on her visit to me, plus one of our own church members, a woman who assisted me from time to time when I was ministering in the realm of the occult, should gather privately in our church one evening for this service of holy communion.

I had explained to the mother that if my 'hunch' was

correct, we were dealing not with an evil spirit but with the living soul of her first child, and I suggested that it would be helpful if she would choose a name, so that we could refer to the soul as a person rather than 'it'. I wrote the name (let's say it was James) on a card, which I placed on the table, together with the bread and wine. I used only the central part of the liturgy of the communion service, and began with a prayer, which went something like this:

> Father, we come to you as your children, and confess that we are not sure what is needed, nor just what we are doing, but something is wrong, and we want to bring you into the situation. We bring before you John and James. Guide us in what we do in this service, and use it to heal John and bring peace and fulfilment to James.

I had already explained to the mother that the abortion of the healthy baby was wrong and, in fact, she needed no convincing, having carried a burden of guilt for many years. At this stage of the service, therefore, she confessed her sin, and asked the Lord to forgive and cleanse her. I pronounced an absolution in terms which were personal to her. I then reminded the Lord that this was the one service he had specifically commanded us to hold in remembrance of him. We believed that he was present with us and would work his perfect will as we reached out to him in faith. I then said the 'words of consecration', we shared in the bread and wine, and I said a final prayer of thanksgiving, followed by the blessing. The whole service had taken less than half an hour.

Although the mother had been very open with me, I knew that she had found the whole matter rather embarrassing and, as I have explained, her husband did not want to be involved, and so, as her home was some way from our parish, I told her that I would leave it to her to contact me if she felt I could be of further assistance. I heard nothing more.

However, about two years or so later, I was at a meeting, and I was introduced to a woman who said, 'You don't remember me, do you?' I had to admit that I did not. It was the mother, who then asked if I recalled the incident involving her son. I assured her I remembered it very well, and asked what had happened. 'He woke up the next morning a different child,' she said, 'and there has been no recurrence of the problem ever since.'

I record that story because it is unusual, at least in my experience, in a number of respects. First, the affected person, the young boy, was totally unaware of the action we had taken, and was not even present at the service – he was asleep in his bed at home.

Second, this was not a case of demonisation. So far as I can know, it was the soul of another human being – the aborted baby. This is the only case in my personal experience where, apparently, a human soul has been involved. In every other case, it has been an evil spirit. I do not believe that evil spirits are the souls of departed people; they are a different species of being. Therefore, in this case, I did not attempt to order 'the spirit' to leave; I simply brought the matter to the Lord for him to deal with.

I remember a strange experience related by a friend of my wife. Her father had recently died, and one night he appeared to her in a dream. From then onwards he appeared every night. She said that it was not an ordinary dream; it was as vivid as a nightmare, but was not as frightening, although it was not particularly pleasant or comforting. In fact it was disturbing because she felt that her father was trying to contact her for some purpose which she could not discern. My wife explained that we do not believe that the dead are able to contact us, and that it was not the spirit of her father at all; if it were anything other than her unconscious mind, it would be some other form of spirit. My wife offered to pray with her, and she readily agreed. Her prayer was basically that the Lord would give her peace and sound sleep, and keep her in safety.

It was about a week before my wife saw her friend again and asked her how she was. She related a strange experience. The night following the prayer, her 'father' had appeared to her again, but this time only half of his face was there; the other half was as though it had been torn away, revealing a sort of skull but with an evil expression. From then onwards, the dream ceased and has never recurred. For myself, and each must interpret it as he or she will, I believe this shows the graciousness of our Lord, who does all things well. Had the dreams just ceased, our friend might always have wondered if it *had* been her father's spirit. As it was, she said to my wife, 'You were right: it wasn't my father; it was evil. I am so glad I know.'

4

Who or What Are Demons?

The scriptural background

In the introduction to Chapter 2, I stated: 'There are some Christians who do not believe in the existence of the devil. They admit that Jesus spoke of him as a reality, but they say that our Lord was a person of his times when it was common to attribute to satanic influence behaviour which today we realise is caused by mental or psychological disorder.' I do not accept that argument, and my experience confirms my belief that there is a difference between healing and deliverance. The Gospels consistently proclaim that Jesus bestowed upon his disciples the same threefold ministry which characterised his own: 'Preach the good news; heal the sick; cast out demons.' On various occasions, the three areas are mentioned in a different order, and on one (Luke 10:8–9), when it appears that Jesus spoke only of healing and preaching, the disciples returned saying, 'Lord, even the demons submit to us in your name' (Luke 10:17). The same threefold ministry appears again in the Great Commission:

> Go into all the world and preach the good news to all creation . . .
> these signs will accompany those who believe: In my name they
> will drive out demons . . . they will place their hands on sick
> people, and they will get well. (Mark 16:15–18)

Scripture makes a clear distinction between sickness and
demonisation, and the reported methods of dealing with the
two are quite different.

It may be helpful if I set out the teaching of Scripture regarding the devil and demons. Each individual must make his or
her own decision as to what they make of this teaching, but
despite references to Satan appearing in different books,
written at different times by different authors, the teaching is
remarkably consistent.

Scripture states clearly that animals and humankind are not
the only forms of thinking beings created by God. It refers to
angels, cherubim and seraphim, powers, world rulers and
spiritual hosts of wickedness. The opening of John's Gospel
assures us that *everything* was created by and through the
Word of God, and without him nothing was made that has
been made. Genesis tells us that everything God made was
'very good' (Genesis 1:31). Indeed, it must have been created
good because his 'eyes are too pure to look on evil'
(Habakkuk 1:13).

It is important to understand this, because it means that as
there is no source of creation other than God, there cannot be
equal and opposing forces of good and evil involved in creation; everything that is came from God. Therefore, if there are
evil beings in existence, they must originally have been good.
The word 'satan' basically means 'adversary', but eventually
it became the proper name of the principal adversary of God
and his ways. It is a mystery why a totally good being should

choose to rebel against its Creator. At first sight, it may seem an equal mystery as to why mankind should rebel. However, there the situation is not quite the same, because by the time mankind was created Satan had already rebelled, and it was he who tempted mankind to sin (as he had already sinned). In Satan's case, there was no prior sin in existence and, therefore, no temptation outside himself.

There are two passages in the Old Testament which may give a hint as to why Satan fell. The first is in Isaiah chapter 14. The prophet is denouncing the king of Babylon, but in the midst of his taunt there is a strange passage, which seems to apply to some being other than a man:

> How you have fallen from heaven, O morning star, son of the dawn! You have been cast down to the earth, you who once laid low the nations! You said in your heart, 'I will ascend to heaven; I will raise my throne above the stars of God; I will sit enthroned on the mount of assembly, on the utmost heights of the sacred mountain. I will ascend above the tops of the clouds; I will make myself like the Most High.' (Isaiah 14:12–14)

The word translated 'morning star' is 'Lucifer' – referring obviously to a being of light.

The other passage is Ezekiel chapter 28. As with Isaiah, the prophet is denouncing a human being, the ruler or prince of Tyre, but he then addresses the 'king' of Tyre in words which seem meaningless if they apply to a man:

> You were the model of perfection, full of wisdom and perfect in beauty. You were in Eden, the garden of God . . . You were anointed as a guardian cherub, for so I ordained you. You were on the holy mount of God; you walked among the fiery stones. You were blameless in your ways from the day you were created

till wickedness was found in you . . . So I drove you in disgrace
from the mount of God, and I expelled you, O guardian cherub . . .
Your heart became proud on account of your beauty, and you cor-
rupted your wisdom because of your splendour. So I threw you to
the earth; I made a spectacle of you before kings. (Ezekiel
28:12–17)

These two passages seem to speak of some spiritual being
behind the human rulers who are addressed – a being of great
splendour and beauty, created to serve in the very presence of
God. Yet somehow pride entered his heart and, discontented
with his position, he sought to challenge God himself.

I am not putting great reliance on the implication, strong as
it may be, that these passages refer to Satan, but draw attention to them as offering a possible explanation as to why a
spiritual being, created 'very good' by a holy God, should
choose to rebel against him – he became proud because of his
beauty.

The unseen spiritual realm

Other references to the devil and different spiritual beings are
far more specific. The book of Daniel lifts the curtain on this
unseen spiritual realm. Daniel was a man who walked closely
with God and who had many visions. On one occasion, he had
a revelation which he could not understand, so he fasted and
meditated in order that he might receive the interpretation of it.
After three weeks, he had another vision, this time of a heavenly
being who recounts a strange story. He says that he was dis-
patched on the very first day that Daniel sought the explanation, in order to reveal it to him. However, he was delayed in
the spiritual realm by 'the prince of the Persian kingdom' for 21

days and apparently he would not have reached Daniel even then had not 'Michael, one of the chief princes' come to help him. All that is recorded in Daniel 10:1–14. A few verses later, he adds some other interesting information: 'Soon I will return to fight against the prince of Persia, and when I go, the prince of Greece will come . . . (No-one supports me against them except Michael, your prince . . .)' (Daniel 10:20–21). That last phrase is amplified later: 'At that time Michael, the great prince who protects your people, will arise' (Daniel 12:1).

Here we have the assertion that there are angels, or spiritual princes, who are in some way responsible for different nations in the world. The one who cares for the people of Israel is an archangel named Michael. Apparently, some of the angels have rebelled and have joined the devil in opposing the holy God who created them.

We find the same picture taken up in the book of Revelation:

> And there was war in heaven. Michael and his angels fought against the dragon, and the dragon and his angels fought back. But he was not strong enough, and they lost their place in heaven. (Revelation 12:7–8)

And, lest there should be any doubt about the identity of the dragon, the writer goes on: 'The great dragon was hurled down – that ancient serpent called the devil, or Satan, who leads the whole world astray. He was hurled to the earth, and his angels with him' (Revelation 12:9).

If we trace this study of Satan and angels through the Bible, we see that there is a carefully detailed hierarchy. Apparently, individuals have 'guardian' angels: 'See that you do not look down on one of these little ones. For I tell you that their angels in heaven always see the face of my Father in heaven'

(Matthew 18:10). And so do churches: 'To the angel of the church in Ephesus write . . .' (Revelation 2:1. See also Revelation 2:8, 12, 18; 3:1, 7, 14).

We have already seen that nations have their princes and there is also a more senior prince still: the prince of this world: 'Now is the time for judgement on this world; now the prince of this world will be driven out' (John 12:31. See also John 14:30; 16:11 and also 2 Corinthians 4:4, Ephesians 2:2 and 1 John 4:4). From the context of these references there can be no doubt that the prince of this world is Lucifer, now known as Satan.

There is a very strange passage in the letter of Jude which has an interesting bearing on all this: 'But even the archangel Michael, when he was disputing with the devil about the body of Moses, did not dare to bring a slanderous accusation against him, but said, "The Lord rebuke you!"' (Jude 9).

The context of that verse is that Jude is warning his readers against godless men who reject authority and slander celestial beings. His argument is that these are mere men who are doing this, whereas even the archangel Michael would not himself dare to make accusations against Satan, but said 'The *Lord* rebuke you!'. The point being, apparently, that although Michael was an archangel, he was responsible for only a nation (albeit that nation is God's own people, the Jews) whereas the devil had been appointed the prince of the whole world, and was thus senior to him.

Incidentally, this throws light on the temptation of Jesus in the wilderness, when Satan offered to give Jesus all the kingdoms of the world:

The devil led him up to a high place and showed him in an instant all the kingdoms of the world. And he said to him, 'I will give you all their authority and splendour, for it has been given to me, and I can give it to anyone I want to. So if you worship me, it will all be yours.' (Luke 4:5–7)

Here, the devil claims that the kingdoms of the world *have been given to him*. This was not a false claim; if it were, all Jesus had to do was to refute it and say that they were not his to give, in which case there would have been no temptation. The fact is that Jesus had come to win the nations, and here was the devil offering to let him have them without him having to go to the cross. It was a very real temptation indeed.

What is more, in one of his letters, John makes a very significant statement: 'We know that we are children of God, and that the whole world is under the control of the evil one' (1 John 5:19). He wrote that after the resurrection and ascension of Jesus. That is to say, we live in a world which even now is under Satan's control. We need to remember that although the devil has been defeated, he has not yet been destroyed. That will happen when Jesus comes again: 'Then the end will come, when he hands over the kingdom to God the Father after he has destroyed all dominion, authority and power' (1 Corinthians 15:24).

Until then, as Paul says: 'Our struggle is not against flesh and blood, but against the rulers, against the authorities, against the powers of this dark world and against the spiritual forces of evil in the heavenly realms' (Ephesians 6:12).

Different spiritual forces

It is interesting that Paul does not say only 'spiritual forces of evil in the heavenly realms', but he differentiates between:

rulers (*arche*), which is the term we have already met – princes with rule over a specific locality or nation; authorities (*exousia*) – those with a freedom of authority, so, apparently, they are not confined to a particular area; powers of this dark world (*kosmokrator*) – world rulers who are obviously very high up in the hierarchy but, as there are more than one of them, they cannot include Satan himself who, as prince of the world, rules over them. It may well be that this is the position, 'world ruler', which the devil offered to Jesus, provided he would change his allegiance and worship him. Finally, there are the spiritual hosts of wickedness, who seem to be the troops serving under these rulers. Very likely, these are the evil spirits we encounter in cases requiring deliverance.

Let me complete this brief survey of the scriptural teaching about the spiritual forces of evil by referring to three other passages. In the story of the temptation of Job, the writer states:

> On another day the angels came to present themselves before the Lord, and Satan also came with them to present himself before him. And the Lord said to Satan, 'Where have you come from?' Satan answered the Lord, 'From roaming through the earth and going to and fro in it.' (Job 2:1–2)

It is not surprising that 'the prince of this world' should have been roaming through the earth, for that was the domain originally given to him when he was an angel of light.

On some occasion in the eternal realm (perhaps after the death, resurrection and ascension of Jesus, i.e. his victory), as we have already seen, the devil and his angels lost their place in heaven and were hurled to the earth (Revelation 12:8–9). In his vision John hears a voice say, among other things:

'Therefore rejoice, you heavens and you who dwell in them! But woe to the earth and the sea, because the devil has gone down to you! He is filled with fury, because he knows that his time is short.' (Revelation 12:12)

The implication behind that verse is clearly that because Satan cannot attack God directly, he will do all he can to wreak havoc on God's creation, especially on mankind, the apple of God's eye. But there is the wonderful statement to give us encouragement that the devil knows that he has only a limited time. That truth is echoed by the words spoken to Jesus by the demons dwelling in the man we know as Legion (although, of course, that was not the man naming himself but the demons speaking through him and, presumably, attempting to intimidate Jesus by claiming that there were a great number of them): ' "What do you want with us, Son of God? they shouted. Have you come here to torture us before the appointed time?" ' (Matthew 8:29).

It seems that the demons, like their master, Satan, are aware that there is an 'appointed time' when they will be destroyed. What surprised them was that Jesus was here confronting them before that time. They were expecting him as King, but were unaware that he would come first, 'veiled in flesh', to be the Saviour of mankind. What is important for us is the fact that we go into battle against an enemy who knows already that he is destined to lose. What a great advantage for us to have.

This brings me to the final verse I would quote. We have seen that John, in his first letter, states that the whole world lies under the control of the evil one, but he does so only after proclaiming another truth: 'You, dear children, are from God and have overcome them, because the one who is in you is greater than the one who is in the world' (1 John 4:4).

We fight against spiritual forces of evil in the heavenly realms, but we do so with the certain knowledge that Jesus is in us and at the name of Jesus every knee must bow, not only on earth, but in heaven and under the earth. So great is the victory Jesus has won.

I am aware that there will be some who will accuse me of taking these texts far too literally. I would repeat my opening comment that each individual must decide what they make of this teaching of Scripture. However, that teaching is astonishingly consistent when we remember that it is found in different contexts across both the Old and New Testaments, from very different authors. I would add that it makes sense within the situations we face in the world of today and, for myself, it fits in with my personal experience of dealing with manifestations of the occult. I do not believe that spirits are persons in the sense that we human beings are persons, but I do believe that they have the ability to think and to express themselves.

In fairness to myself, I should mention that although I find this scriptural perspective useful and effective in the practice of deliverance, I do not hold such a rigid understanding of evil spirits in my personal belief. Scripture speaks of God's eyes, his arms, his hands and his feet, yet God is spirit and has no body as we understand it. It has to speak in such terms because we are familiar with them, and they are tools to help us comprehend something which is, in fact, beyond our comprehension. They are rather like scaffolding used while constructing a building, which, when the building is complete, is removed. The biblical description of demons may be similar, using terms familiar to us but which are not intended to be taken entirely literally, although, nevertheless, they relate to something very real.

5

Ministering Deliverance

I have probably given enough background information to turn now to giving some details of how to set about delivering a person who is demonised. Let me say again that these can only be general guidelines, because we need to be open to the leading of the Holy Spirit.

Although it may be stating the obvious, it is essential that the person who is ordering the deliverance should be walking with the Lord. To seek to rid a person of demonic influence is to declare war in the spiritual realm, and the powers of darkness are reluctant to yield. They have to do so at the name of Jesus, provided we are trusting in that name, but they can pick up very quickly whether or not we are truly trusting in it. The story recounted in Acts 19:13–16, when the sons of a Jewish chief priest attempted to cast out an evil spirit in the name of Jesus, should be a warning. The demonised man jumped on them and beat them up after the spirit had answered, 'Jesus I know, and I know about Paul, but who are you?'

The need for authority

A friend of mine told me of an interesting experience he'd had when he first began to minister in this field. My friend had been seeking to help a man who was obviously troubled by evil spirits. Because of his inexperience, it was taking longer than it should have done. Both he and the man became very tired; indeed, the man actually fell asleep. My friend decided to take the opportunity to get some rest himself. He instructed a young colleague who was there to assist him that should the man wake up and begin to manifest in some way, he should simply say, 'Be still in the name of the Lord Jesus'. Then he went into another room to recuperate. After a while, the man did wake up, and began to advance on the young colleague, who stood up and, in some panic, stammered, 'Be still in the name of Jesus.' The man continued to advance, and the colleague began to back away, still mumbling, 'Be still in the name of Jesus.' In the end, he took flight and rushed to get my friend, who faced the man and repeated the same words, 'In the name of Jesus, be still.' However, *he* spoke them with authority and without fear. Immediately, the man returned to his seat.

It is both pointless and dangerous to attempt deliverance unless we are utterly convinced for ourselves that Jesus is Lord of all and that at his name every knee must bow.

Some who are involved in this ministry advocate a time of both prayer and fasting before entering upon it on every separate occasion. This is obviously in response to the comment of Jesus when he was casting a spirit out of a young lad after his disciples had failed to do so. When they asked why they had been unable to deal with the situation, Jesus explained that this sort comes out only by prayer and fasting (Mark

9:29). (Incidentally, many manuscripts omit the words 'and fasting'.) Far be it from me to say that to fast before attempting to minister is wrong – anything which strengthens us spiritually is surely beneficial and, on occasions, I have done this myself. However, notice that Jesus was suddenly confronted by this situation; he had no time specifically to pray and fast before casting out the spirit. I believe that what Jesus was explaining here was that we should be living a holy life, walking with God all the time, which will involve prayer and fasting, irrespective of whether we know when we will be confronted with a case requiring deliverance.

First, of course, the sufferer must truly and totally desire to be delivered. Here let me expand on the case I mentioned in the introduction to this book.

The man with a spirit of death

A man, whose mother had been a spiritist medium, apparently had been born with an infestation of spirits within him. He was very intelligent and had entered one of the professions requiring years of study and training, but he had never known what it was to be totally free. He was a member of our congregation and came to me seeking help. It was the first time I had been personally involved in a case of deliverance, and I approached a colleague in a neighbouring parish, who had had considerable experience in this field. It was he who actually conducted the deliverance, and I assisted by praying while it was going on and observed what he did.

In the course of ministering to this man, my colleague 'uncovered' a spirit of death. (I will speak further about this later.) He commanded it to leave, which it seemed to do, only to return a few minutes later. (Here I should explain that evil spirits seem to dwell in packs. It may be helpful to speak of 'a' spirit of death, but to bear in mind that there will almost certainly be quite a number of spirits with the same attributes involved. It could well have been, therefore, that one or more spirits of death had left, but others remained. However, in this case I 'sensed' that this was not so.) I was convinced that there was something that was allowing the spirit(s) of death to return. I had the impression that they were hooked onto something within the man, and were leaving at the name of Jesus, only to spring back as though attached by elastic. I shared this with my colleague, who was grateful for the suggestion. This is one of the benefits of having two or more people involved; while one is concentrating on ministering the deliverance, the others are, perhaps, more free to receive prompting from the Holy Spirit.

As he continued the ministry, I received further revelation. I realised that life was often such a torment for this man that in the back of his mind there was the thought, which he hardly admitted to himself, that if it became too unbearable he could always commit suicide. I shared this and asked him if it were true. The man thought about it and confessed that there had been times when he had contemplated the possibility of ending his life, and so it was very likely true that in his unconscious he was harbouring this final way out. On the instructions of my colleague, he confessed his sin of holding on to the escape of suicide, repented and asked the Lord's forgiveness. This time, when my friend commanded every spirit of death to leave, it did so and did not return. As I say, it is important that the person seeking deliverance totally desires this and is not allowing an evil spirit any hold to hook in to.

It is also very important to check whether he or she has been involved with the occult – seances, Ouija board, etc., as detailed in Chapter 1. Witchcraft and Satanism cause particular difficulties. It is vital that repentance and confession is made, otherwise the evil spirits will not leave.

A spiritual hierarchy

I have found that, in line with the implication in Scripture, there seems to be a hierarchy of spirits. In speaking of the cleansing of places, I mentioned that spirits which indwell people are usually greater and more powerful than those involved in the disturbance of places. That statement requires clarification. Very often, in the case of people, when I begin to minister to them the first manifestation (assuming that there *is* some demonisation present) is a spirit of mockery, confusion or disruption.

Perhaps I should explain that occasionally the spirit(s) will actually speak audibly *from* the person but, more frequently, they will speak *to or within* the person, who is then able to explain what they are saying, or what is happening in his or her mind. Were they not so intrinsically evil, what these 'lesser' spirits say or do would be laughable. At the command that they are to go, the 'patient' may have the mental impression of something like the proscenium arch of a theatre, with the spirit putting its 'head' round the edge, saying, 'I've gone; I really have gone.' The behaviour is similar to that of children who are too young to appreciate that their statements are illogical. They may even indulge in a sort of pantomime conversation of the 'oh yes there is, oh no there isn't' variety. I realise that in the past I often spent much unnecessary time seeking to 'cast out' these spirits.

I now believe that this is indeed the purpose of their behaviour – to waste time and to create a distraction. These are not the real cause of the patient's distress; they are simply the first ones to surface. Underneath, and deeper within the person, there is likely to be something far more serious. I understand that whales have around them what are called 'pilot fish', which are very small, and which have learned that medium-sized fish, which might well prey on them, will not come near to the whale lest they, in turn, become *its* prey. I think of these spirits of mockery and the like as similar to pilot fish. I have found that it is often helpful to make it clear that I am fully aware of the tactic, that I have no intention of spending time with these minions, and that I know there is a far greater spirit which is seeking to hide behind these stupid manifestations.

Fairly recently, I had some degree of confirmation of my understanding that there are these 'lesser spirits' surrounding the more dangerous ones.

The case of the 'munchkins'

Late one evening, I was telephoned by a man I had known, on and off, over a number of years. He was a believer but had rather gone off the rails. He was in some distress, and told me that over the past two weeks his wife of some two years had developed disturbing symptoms, showing short bouts of great antagonism towards him, even to hitting him in the face and speaking abusively, and then returning to her normal self. With great difficulty, over a period of some days, she had told him that as a child she had been repeatedly raped. She had never spoken of it to anyone before. As so often in these cases, although she was the victim, she felt guilty. She was being attacked by the apparition of some spirit, which laughed at her and told her she would never be able to rid herself of it, and which was encouraging her to attack and to leave her husband. Apparently, she could see this apparition at the time her husband was phoning me; he had never seen it.

Over the two weeks, he had played Christian music tapes and prayed which, according to her, made the apparition decrease in size. That evening, things had reached a climax; he was emotionally drained and, in desperation, telephoned me for advice as to what he should do to get through the night. I could hear her crying in the background, and I was concerned that he might stir things up even more. As they lived not too far away, I agreed to visit them there and then.

I won't go into great detail about what I was able to elicit from her. Suffice it to say that she did manifest demonic oppression, one aspect of which was suddenly to abuse her husband verbally and then immediately change her whole manner and apologise, saying that she hadn't wanted to say what she had.

The interesting aspect of this case was that it seems that the apparition was a sort of projection of something that was, in fact, inside her – similar to the way that a film in a projector is thrown onto a screen. I told them that I believed that while there was some spiritual dimension to her problem, she would also need medical or psychiatric help, which she must seek. They both agreed to do this.

There was no time, nor was she in a fit state, for me to gather all the detailed information I usually like to have, but I could not just walk out, leaving her in such distress, so I decided to take emergency action to get the thing to disclose something of itself, to give me an indication of the action required. I was encouraged in that usually a spirit will seek to hide, and its presence is only revealed by irrational behaviour on the part of the victim, when there is then the problem of deciding if it is mental, spiritual, or a combination of the two.

In this case it was clearly near the surface. I was aware that I was dealing with a woman, and I had no female assistance. However, the husband was there and imploring me to help, and he was someone I knew. The woman made one interesting request – in ministering to her, would I please not make the sign of the cross. In the past, when a spirit has sought to hide, I have found that making the sign of the cross over the person is a most effective way of causing it to panic and reveal its presence. Her very request seemed an additional confirmation of demonic influence.

Then she volunteered further information, which is the point of my recounting this particular case. She told me that the apparition was present at that moment in a corner of the room, laughing at her, and around it were other 'things' which, she said, 'I call munchkins'. On questioning her further, she explained that they seemed to be 'attendant spirits', related in some way to the main one. They were annoying, but did not instil the same fear in her that their master spirit did. It occurred to me at the time that for someone who was as terrified and distressed as she was then, 'munchkins' was a remarkably kind description.

I took authority in the name of Jesus over every spirit that was contrary to the Holy Spirit and, after quoting appropriate passages of Scripture, commanded it to leave. As I was ministering, she said, 'It is getting smaller and smaller.' I explained that the size was not important, but that it had to go completely, and said simply, 'In the name of Christ, come out now.' As frequently happens, the woman reacted as though she were about to vomit, then put her hand over her mouth and said, 'It exploded; as you spoke, it simply exploded. It has gone. I feel and know it has gone.' Apparently the 'munchkins' went with it. She was very grateful, and hung onto my hand so firmly that I had difficulty in disentangling myself. I must admit she appeared to be a totally different person from the one I had met as I entered the room. After a prayer of blessing, and before leaving, I warned the husband that these things have a tendency to hunt in packs and to be on his guard.

I do not wish to be too specific because, as I have said already, each case differs from others. Nevertheless it seems that when I adopt the approach I have described of making it clear that I am not wasting time on the 'munchkins', the greater, more powerful, more senior spirits understand that their cover is blown. In the same way that, as I have explained, they seem to know if I truly believe that I come in the power and with the authority of the Lord Jesus Christ, so they know that I am aware of their presence behind these smaller and somewhat foolish spirits. It is at this stage that things may become far more serious and unpleasant. The patient may show greater signs of distress and internal struggle. If I spend time dealing with the lesser, mischievous spirits, the greater ones simply lie low so that they will not reveal their presence, but when I come directly against *them* in the name of our Lord Jesus Christ, they no longer seek to hide; the activity of the smaller spirits is cast aside, and they take over the battle 'personally', if that term is applicable. In very serious cases they will actually override the patient's consciousness, putting them into a sort of trance, and later, when the deliverance is over, the person may ask what has been happening, because they have been totally unaware. I will give an illustration of this later in the chapter.

These greater spirits will reveal great anger and hatred against the person ministering deliverance. Usually they will claim that they have too much power to have to obey any command to go. The patient can very quickly lose heart at this, and it is important to encourage them and maintain their confidence in the power of Jesus. The spirits will fling insults, such as that the minister is ignorant of the spiritual realm and has no idea what he or she is doing. It is important that the minister is not diverted into any form of argument but maintains a quiet but very firm and clear authority, saying something along the lines of, 'I come in the name of the Lord Jesus Christ: you face him who is the victorious Son of God and at his name every knee must bow. You are subject to him and have to yield at his name.' There is no need to shout; the spirits seem to be more aware of the authority and confidence of the minister than how loudly he or she is speaking.

Almost certainly at some stage the spirits will seek to undermine the confidence of the minister, claiming that he or she has no right to use the name of Jesus. They may even reveal surprising knowledge of the minister's life and refer (in my experience, in a general manner rather than specific detail) to sins he or she has committed. This, as it is intended to be, can be very unnerving. Again, it is vital that the minister is not distracted. I usually respond to this sort of attack with even greater authority, saying, 'How dare you speak like that; I stand in the righteousness of Jesus Christ, cleansed by his blood, and in his name I command that you leave.' Once again, the key to victory here is the shield of faith. Of course, it would be foolish and dangerous to enter into this ministry if there is any known and unconfessed sin on the part of the minister, but the certainty of our salvation forms an effective helmet to protect our minds when spirits seek to undermine our confidence in this way. If the minister is of the opposite sex to the patient, it is very common for the spirits to make allegations of a sexual nature. 'I know why you are doing this. You want her for yourself; you are lusting for her.' Incidentally, this is one reason why it is so important that the minister does not attempt deliverance alone, and that at least one of his or her assistants is of the opposite sex, not least to witness to the propriety of what is going on.

It is essential that the minister and those assisting are not thrown by this tactic. Our only weapon is faith; it is not a matter of skill, nor of experience, although the latter is, of course, useful. The victory is obtained only through faith; that is to say, we must be convinced of the fact that we are loved by God, belong to him, and have been given authority to use the name of Jesus. Like Peter walking on the water, our eyes must be on Jesus, and if we are diverted to consider our own worthiness or lack of it, we shall immediately begin to sink.

Do spirits exhibit intelligence?

I should mention that while the minions may exhibit little intelligence, this is not the case with the more 'senior' spirits. I have discovered that when I make an appointment to meet with someone requiring deliverance, it is important that they and I, and anyone else involved, pray that nothing will prevent the meeting taking place. These evil powers seem to be aware of the situation and will endeavour to intervene. On one occasion, when a particularly powerful spiritual force was involved, I was called urgently to meet with the patient to whom I had been ministering in an ongoing situation. I arranged to call on them that evening. About half an hour before I was due to set off, my wife was taken ill and begged me not to leave her. I telephoned to cancel the appointment and, within a further half hour or so, she had completely recovered. One incident like that might be a coincidence, but it has happened far too often in my experience for me not to take the matter seriously.

If it is possible to do so, I like to meet with a person requiring deliverance on church premises. Not only do I feel this is home ground rather than an 'away match', but we are less likely to be disturbed if there is a separate chapel which is enclosed and with its own door. Alternatively, the vestry may be very suitable, especially if it can be heated, as ministering in a freezing church has no particular virtue, and it simply provides an unnecessary distraction. It is also helpful if toilet facilities are available.

Of course, it is good if I can meet with the person involved before the deliverance, but this is often not practicable. It may be that they live some distance away and have to find someone who can provide transport. In most dioceses, the 'Bishop's Instructions' state that individuals should not be instructed to approach directly the minister who has the bishop's authority to officiate in this field; it is the responsibility of the incumbent to consult the individual. This is important for two reasons: first, it is the incumbent who is involved in the ongoing pastoral care of his or her parishioner and, second, it would be wrong for anyone living anywhere within the diocese who thinks he or she may be under demonic attack to contact the advising minister whenever they feel like it. I remember one particular person who was severely mentally disturbed, who obtained my telephone number and rang me whenever she believed that she was possessed by a demon. I met with her and her family once, and we were all (apart from her) convinced that it was entirely a mental problem, for which she was already being treated by her doctor. She rang me on and off for a number of years. I felt desperately sorry for her, but there was nothing I could do.

As it is the 'patient's' incumbent who makes the initial approach, he or she is able to give a great deal of background information, which will help us decide whether or not I should become involved. However, irrespective of how much or little I have been told about someone, when I meet up with them I will always question them in detail regarding first the symptoms and then the circumstances of their life – have they or any member of the family been involved in the occult, etc.? – very similar to the sort of questions I ask regarding the cleansing of places. Even if I have much of this information already, the manner in which the person gives it – whether they are open or reluctant, and whether they become distressed or agitated while describing particular events – can be very helpful in assessing the situation. Of course, I will have prayed about our meeting beforehand, but I do not always start our time together with a prayer. In some cases where there is demonisation, a prayer may cause the spirit to manifest by putting the person into a form of trance. This has the advantage that it is immediately clear that deliverance is needed, but it puts them 'out' before I have had the opportunity to discover the background as to how they became affected in the first place.

The woman involved in Satanism

One of the most serious and difficult cases I have met arose very suddenly. Two college students, girls who were themselves believers, and one of whom was a member of our congregation, telephoned to say that another student friend of theirs had just confessed that she was deeply involved in Satanism and would like to get out of it; could they bring her to see me immediately? Apparently, it was the last day of term and several of them had gone to a nearby pub to have a celebration drink. Although by no means drunk, her tongue had been sufficiently loosened for her to share as she had with her two friends, and she said that she would be willing to meet with me. They felt it important that I should see her while she was willing for ministry. I happened to be free and I agreed. I just had time to telephone our curate, to ask him to come immediately to join my wife and myself.

When the three of them arrived at the door, the girl involved in Satanism, whom I will call Eve, decided that she didn't want to come in after all. I suggested that as she had come all that way it seemed a shame not to talk, even if we did nothing else, and eventually she consented.

However, hardly had the six of us sat down and I had asked her what she was concerned about, than she said that she didn't want to discuss it and would leave. Of course, I had no right to keep her against her will, so I agreed that she should leave, but just before she went I asked her to let me pray, and without waiting for her response, I launched into a prayer. I cannot recall what I said because immediately I began her whole demeanour changed: she became rigid and both her hands took on a peculiar configuration; the two middle fingers and thumb were folded into the palms, leaving the first and little fingers extended. Later, I learned that this depicts the 'horned god' and was apparently a defence against Christian activity. She appeared to be in a form of trance; her eyelids were closed and, when she did not respond when I asked her to open them, I gently pulled them up to find her eyes were looking upward, as though into her forehead. By speaking normally to her and using her name, I finally managed to get a response, and began to question her. Although she was no longer in a trance, she seemed to be not entirely with us; but this may have been due, at least partly, to the drink she had consumed. She was reluctant to answer my questions, but eventually agreed to tell one of the girls some facts if the rest of us would leave the room. I must admit I was concerned about this, but we were only just outside the door, and when Eve had finished her explanations the friend called us back in and, with Eve's permission, repeated what she had told her. Together with what we discovered as the session continued, her story was as follows.

When she was at school, a teacher had introduced Eve to the occult. At college, she had met up with those involved in witchcraft, black magic and, finally, Satanism. In the course of this, she had renounced her Christian baptism, which had taken place as an infant, and had undergone a satanic baptism, in which she had been given a secret satanic name. Her involvement culminated in her going through a ceremony in which she was married to Satan. Members of the Satanic Society at college had a staged a contest to test who had the greatest powers. She had selected a particular student in whom, she claimed, she would bring about a complete nervous breakdown simply by projecting her thought against him. Within a term she had succeeded, and the student had had to withdraw from college. As a result of this, she had won the contest and had been made the high priestess of the 'coven', if that is the right description.

Shortly before coming to see us, she had been at home one evening, sitting in a chair; the next thing she knew was that although she was still in the room, her shoes and tights were wet through, and the clock showed that two hours had passed. Obviously she had been out, but she had no idea where she had been or what she had done in that time. She was frightened because she realised that she had had no control over herself and, for all she knew, might well have committed a crime. It was this fear which, when she had had a couple of drinks, had encouraged her to speak to her friends about wanting to 'get out'. However, she was also very afraid of the others in the coven. She claimed that they would very soon be aware if she attempted to withdraw. She claimed also that they would bring spiritual pressure to bear upon her, much in the way that Christians pray for others. The great difference being, of course, that those involved in black magic and Satanism jealously preserve the utmost secrecy, and members must not be allowed to leave, in case they divulge information which could cause the group serious problems.

This was very early in my experience of cases of the paranormal, and I was unsure exactly how to proceed. However, in the course of the next two hours or so I learned a great deal. Over that period a whole range of events happened. I persuaded Eve to renounce her satanic baptism (although we had great difficulty in encouraging her to be willing to divulge her satanic name) and asked her to call upon the name of Jesus. Her speech became confused and she kept repeating what sounded like the word 'Sausage'. I suddenly realised that she was pronouncing 'Jesus' backwards. I produced a Bible and asked her to read a passage from the Gospels. Again she read all the words backwards and at an astonishing speed. Unless she had deliberately practised reading in this manner, which seems unlikely, there was something very unusual in her ability to do this. Although I tried to get her to read forwards in the normal manner, she was apparently unable to do so.

I then came against whatever power was in her and commanded in the name of Jesus that it should depart. This had an effect which I found profoundly unnerving. Eve fell to the floor and lay on her back with her eyes closed, completely rigid. For a moment, it crossed my mind that she was dead.

Speaking to her, or shaking her gently, prompted no response at all. I was deeply concerned. Then, for some reason, which I now believe was the prompting of the Holy Spirit, I stood over her and made the sign of the cross virtually over the whole length of her body. The effect was immediate and violent: she uttered what I can describe only as a roar of anger, and began to thrash out with her arms. After a while, this ceased and for the rest of the time we were ministering to her she did not relapse into such a 'trance' again. However, this was followed by another frightening incident. Eve was sitting facing me, with one of her friends and our curate sitting on either side. I was asking questions when suddenly her de-meanour changed. I can say only that I saw something in her eyes and 'knew' what was about to happen. I just had time to shout 'hold her', which the friend and curate did immediately, when she stood up and a voice, coming from her, screamed 'kill her' and she put her head down and tried to run hard into the wall behind me. Very fortunately, although she showed surprising strength and the two holding her were pulled forward, they managed to restrain her before she could harm herself in any way.

In the course of my questioning her, her voice changed to that of a man. It was as though her own personality had been bypassed and whatever was in her took over control. I had the impression that the spirit decided that she could not be trusted to withstand such spiritual attack from a Christian and deter-mined to deal with me direct. The spirit, still speaking in a deep, male voice, claimed that 'he' had been invited to enter and refused to leave. Quietly but persistently I commanded that in the name of Jesus it had to go, and eventually it did so, with a loud scream. The experience felt to me similar to tearing out a very deeply embedded weed in a garden.

For a while, Eve sat quietly in a chair, and I was hopeful that the deliverance was complete and she simply needed time to recover. Deliverance can be a very exhausting experience for the person involved – and also for those who do the ministering. However, Eve began to speak again, this time in a sing-song voice. This spirit claimed to be a cat-spirit and, at the same time, Eve began to move her head in a way similar to that of a cat rubbing its head against a chair leg. Again, after some time of commanding it to leave, it did so, once more with a scream.

Later, Eve told us that in order to gain more and more power she had invited certain spirits to enter her. Apparently, Satanists have lists of different spirits with specific powers, and she had carefully selected the ones she desired, one of which was indeed a cat-spirit, which she mentioned by name – although I cannot now recall what that was.

In the course of ministering to her for well over two hours, we were able to deliver her from three distinct spirits. I was by no means sure that she was entirely free, but I was convinced that she had had quite enough for one afternoon, and so had I. She was very much calmer than when she had arrived, and seemed grateful for what we had been able to do, but I was very concerned about what should happen next. She needed help – more than we could give. Fortunately, a few miles away there was a Christian organisation with facilities for helping young people withdraw from drugs. They had accommodation, with staff who provided a round-the-clock watch on their patients. This work had brought them into contact with many who had been involved with the occult, and they agreed to accept her into care.

Let me say that I am not proud of the way I handled this matter, and certainly I am recording it not as an illustration of best practice but because of the insight it gives, both into what can happen when people become attracted to the occult and what may be happening in our colleges regarding the occult. When I was on the course I have mentioned, organised by the Bishop of Exeter's Commission on Exorcism, I met up with someone who specialised in helping young people involved with the occult. He claimed that those within witchcraft, black magic and Satanism had a carefully planned structure, with a representative in every major college and university in the country. I have no means of checking that statement, but he was attending that course because of his work in that field.

In setting up a meeting, I like to allow a period of up to three hours – not because I believe it always takes that long, but I have no idea how much background information will be given. It may be that I will have to give a certain amount of counselling, in the light of the information provided, before attempting any deliverance – if, indeed, deliverance is needed at all. Also, it is important that we can all be as relaxed as possible. If the person involved is anxious about having to meet a child from school or keep some other appointment, this will inevitably create pressure and tension.

Assuming that it does seem probable that deliverance is appropriate, I will first lead the person through any repentance that may be needed. This is not simply with regard to any dabbling in the occult (regarding which I will lead them through confession in the same way as I have described in the case of the cleansing of places) but there may well be someone – often a parent – whom they have never forgiven. There may well be other sins to be confessed. If someone is holding on to unconfessed sin, or a sinful habit of lifestyle, this will provide an area which evil spirits can hook in to, so to speak, and refuse to leave.

The man who had to forgive his mother

On one occasion, I was contacted by the warden of a home for offenders. It was a place where men released from prison could go for a period, while they became acclimatised to life outside and looked for a job and accommodation. He told me that one of the residents had manifested signs of what he thought might well be demonic activity, and he had expressed his desire to be set free. I called at the home and met with the man, together with the staff. In this case I 'felt' it right, before concentrating specifically on the occult, to question him closely about his relationship with his mother when he was a child. Although at first he spoke about her more or less reasonably, it soon became apparent that he carried a strong resentment towards her. From what he told me it emerged that she was either a prostitute or had lived with a variety of different men. He did not know who was his father. As he spoke, it became obvious that he harboured far more than resentment; he was eaten up with bitterness because he believed, rightly or wrongly, that his mother had neglected him. It needed few questions on my part for it all to come tumbling out. I spent a considerable amount of time counselling him, encouraging him to let go all his pain of rejection. I think what carried the greatest influence was when I explained to him that he was not hurting his mother with the great weight of anger and resentment he was carrying, but he most certainly was hurting himself. She wasn't even aware of the feelings which were holding him in bondage. Eventually, he was able to let it all go. He recognised and confessed his feelings to be sin, and I was then able to offer him absolution.

He was indeed demonised, but his deliverance was comparatively easy and quick. Although I cannot prove it, I am convinced that this was because he was now in a state of grace, and the bitterness and unforgiveness he had been nurturing had formed a fruitful soil in which the spirits would have been able to be rooted had I attempted the deliverance before dealing with his deep and wrongly directed emotions.

Working with the medical profession

Most 'Bishop's Instructions', and certainly those of my own diocese, lay down that in conducting deliverance the minister should work in close co-operation with the medical profession. I believe that this is a wise provision, but I have discovered that in practice it is not always one possible to observe. Very often the situation requiring deliverance ministry arises as an emergency. The case I have already related of the 'munchkins' illustrates this. A telephone call at 11 pm from someone in extreme distress means that it will be impossible to contact their doctor immediately – in our area, a telephone call to the doctor at that time of night will be handled by a central registry, who will contact a locum. Rightly or wrongly, I cannot always bring myself to tell a person in such immediate panic and distress, 'I will deal with the matter in the morning.' They are seeking and needing help from Christ's church then and there. Having said that, it often transpires that the problem has been present for a considerable period beforehand, but something has occurred which terrifies them – often late at night – and drives them to seek immediate help. With regard to the cleansing of places, I will very often tell them I will visit the next day, but with deliverance, although I may attempt to delay, the situation may be rather more dangerous, and it may be advisable to get there as soon as possible.

However, if I cannot contact their doctor first, I will question the patient carefully about their medical condition, whether they are receiving treatment or are taking any medication or drugs. Also, in many cases – as in the 'munchkins' one – I will strongly advocate that they should contact their doctor as soon as possible.

There is another problem, also. In my experience, although many GPs are sympathetic to working with clergy, the majority of psychiatrists are not – particularly in the realm of deliverance; they do not accept the concept of evil spirits. This proved a particular problem in one case where I was consulted, although it was not directly a psychiatrist who caused it.

The case of the fostered children

A vicar asked me to call on a couple of his parishioners who were active members of his congregation. They fostered children and were particularly highly regarded by the local authority in handling difficult ones. They had been asked to take in two young brothers who had been causing problems in school and who had been transferred from another authority in a different part of the country.

The foster parents had become concerned because the two behaved so strangely at times, casting 'spells' on anyone who upset them. On one occasion, the husband had told off the elder brother (who was under ten) for some misdemeanour and then gone out somewhere in his car. After a while, the young lad, at home in the house with the wife, showed signs of great agitation, explaining that in his anger (at being rebuked) he had put some influence over her husband. He was now sorry about it, but couldn't withdraw it, and was deeply worried at what might happen to the man. When the husband came home, it was to report that his car had spontaneously caught fire when it was parked at the roadside; fortunately, he was not in it at the time.

The foster parents realised that it could have been coincidence, but there had been other similar incidents which caused them concern. The children spoke of peculiar things which their previous foster parents had done, and which caused the couple who had called me in to wonder if they had been involved in witchcraft or Satanism. They had noticed, to their surprise, that when the boys arrived, every single item of clothing they brought with them was black.

I had, and have, never conducted deliverance of a child. (Earlier, I have recorded holding a service of holy communion 'with intent', in the case of the boy who appeared to be sharing his life with his aborted brother; but in that case it was the mother who was present, while the boy himself was in bed at home.) I told the foster parents that I would only consider meeting to talk with the boys, let alone attempt any deliverance which might seem appropriate, with the full approval of the authorities responsible for placing the boys in foster care, and I would require one of their representatives to be in attendance to observe what happened throughout the whole meeting. I felt this was essential to avoid any repercussions or false allegations about what I had or had not done.

It so happened that the officer overseeing this particular placement was herself a Christian, and was very sympathetic to the views of the foster parents. However, she said that she could not possibly approach her superiors at that time because she knew that they would completely dismiss any ideas of the occult. And so I never met with the boys.

I recount that story not because I can vouch for the truth of the suppositions but because it illustrates the difficulty of working with those whose approach is totally unsympathetic to any belief in the spiritual realm. Having said that, this case arose not long after the media had given extensive coverage to claims that fostered and adopted children were being used by their parents in occult activities on one of the Scottish islands; claims which were later declared to be false, and which involved the social services in much criticism and distress. So it is not surprising if the local authority in this case would have been wary.

All I could do was point out that if it were indeed true that the brothers had been subjected to occult influence through their previous foster parents, then the Lord was stronger than the enemy, and just by living in a Christian home his influence could overcome the evil of the past. What is more, the authorities were fully aware that the couple were Christians, so they were at liberty to share their beliefs with the boys and to pray with them, as indeed they had been doing, not only with these two but with all the children they had fostered previously. I gather that over a number of months the boys' behaviour did improve. However, eventually the authorities decided to make alternative arrangements for them, and they left the care of this couple.

Apart from Dr Ken McCall, whom I have already mentioned as a member of the Bishop of Exeter's Commission, I personally have met up with only one other psychiatrist who was prepared to believe that occult oppression of a patient might be a possibility.

The 'gifted' customs officer

One afternoon, I was telephoned by a junior doctor at one of our local hospitals. He had recently qualified and was completing his training by spending a number of weeks on different wards. Currently, he was serving in the psychiatric wing. He explained that he was himself a Christian, and that afternoon he had come across a patient on the day ward (i.e. attending during the day but sleeping at home) whose symptoms did not fit totally within the normal mental disorders he had encountered previously. He believed that this man was under some form of spiritual oppression and had raised this possibility with the consultant psychiatrist, suggesting that it might be helpful to call in a clergyman; the consultant had given his permission. Someone had given the young doctor my name, and he asked if I was free to go to the hospital then and there to meet with him and his patient.

When I arrived, the doctor gave me something of the background. Apparently, the patient, whom I will call George, was a customs officer. He had discovered that he had the 'gift' of being able to recognise people who were attempting to smuggle goods into the country. Looking at the crowds passing through, he just 'knew' which people to approach to search their baggage. All good customs officers develop a certain skill in this regard, but in his case it was more than a skill; he just 'knew' within him. He became very successful at his job.

In addition, he discovered he had two other 'gifts'. First, he was able to foresee or foretell certain events relating to the family before they happened. On one occasion, his wife discovered him lighting the fire in their front room on a weekday evening, although they only used that room at the weekends. He explained, 'Oh, so and so is coming round to see us this evening.' But nothing had been arranged; George just 'knew' within him that this visitor would arrive – which he did. The other 'gift' was that he was able to 'send' a message and influence people just by thought. On his way home, he would project a thought to his wife to make a cup of tea. She was not aware of receiving the message, but when he arrived home she would say, 'Oh, you're just in time for a cup of tea. I've just made one.'

He had enjoyed using his 'gifts', and had sought to develop them. However, over the immediately preceding weeks he had felt that instead of him controlling his gifts, they had begun to control him, and he found himself doing things he had neither intended nor wished to do. He felt he was losing control of his mind and had visited his doctor who, in turn, had referred him to the consultant psychiatrist. Having given me this background, the young doctor took me to meet George in a private room. I began to chat to him, asking various questions – particularly about any involvement in seances, Ouija boards, etc., but he denied having any such connections.

As I continued to probe, he said to me, 'It's rather strange; I know you are talking to me, but I cannot distinguish any words.' I had not encountered this before but, once again, I can say only that I knew what I should do; the guidance, I believe, of the Holy Spirit, as Dom Robert had foretold – 'You will know at the time what to do; you will know at the time.' I immediately changed the subject and, it being summer time, asked if George had had a holiday yet. He blinked as though re-establishing his concentration and said, 'What? Oh no, not yet.' I asked if he had one planned and, as he began to chat quite normally again, without giving him any warning I said with authority, 'I come in the name of the Lord Jesus Christ against any spirit contrary to the Holy Spirit of God – out now!' George gave a sudden shout and almost fell out of his chair. Then he asked, 'What was that? What happened?'

Here let me comment, as I have mentioned already, evil spirits often seem to display the attributes of naughty children. As I was questioning George, I had obviously been getting too close for their comfort. In the case of Eve, reported above, they had simply put her right out in a form of trance, but with George they had blanked out his comprehension, so that he could hear my voice but not my words. When I spoke of every-day things, like his summer holiday, they had relaxed and allowed him to regain control of his mind. My sudden switch to commanding them to depart in the name of Jesus had taken them by surprise.

George required ongoing counselling over a period of months, and I was very careful to keep the consultant psychi-atrist advised by letter of what transpired. It was only after some time that it occurred to me that he never replied in writing; he always answered me by telephone. I can only assume that, professionally, he did not wish to set down in a letter his side of the exchange, in case a colleague should inspect the file and, perhaps, ask questions about his belief in the occult. However, he was most courteous in all his dealings and treated me as an equal, another professional working in a different area of healing and wholeness. I discovered later that he was a practising Buddhist, and so, while his faith dif-fered substantially from my own, he accepted the reality of a spiritual realm. Often in our telephone conversations, follow-ing a letter from me explaining a course of action I proposed to take and asking for his comments, he would tell me, 'I think you are probably on the right lines, but that is your realm rather than mine; I leave it to you.'

After a number of weeks, he telephoned me to say that George was so improved that he was planning to discharge him and allow him to return to work, and kindly invited me to meet with himself and the young doctor, together with George, for the final interview. I wish that it were always pos-sible to deal with cases of deliverance on a similar basis of trust and respect. Unfortunately, I have met other psychiatrists who treat me with a patronising smile and scarcely concealed contempt that anyone should be so naïve as to believe in evil spirits. This is sad, not because it belittles me and my own profession, but because it may deprive a patient of the benefits which the two disciplines working in co-operation may afford.

With regard to George, I would record three interesting details. Although he had not been involved in any overt occult activity which might have accounted for his 'gifts', it transpired that he was descended from Romany stock from central Europe. As I have already mentioned with regard to the cleansing of places, Romanies often inherit psychic abilities. In George's case, his deliberate attempt to develop his 'gifts' eventually led to him being controlled by them.

Second, in the course of continuing ministry, George shared on one occasion that as I had prayed with him he had been aware in his mind of something rather like a tiger pacing up and down, and seeking to get at him, but being prevented by a circle of some form of defence around him. I shared with him the words of Scripture: 'Your enemy the devil prowls around like a roaring lion looking for someone to devour' (1 Peter 5:8).

He was not a religious man and had not been aware of that text before. The other very interesting incident was this. About ten days after I first met with George at the hospital, I was visiting at his home. His wife told me that their daughter, who was in her twenties and no longer lived with them, had telephoned her mother to ask what had happened to her father. George's wife explained that they had not told the daughter that her father was having psychiatric treatment; in fact, they were rather embarrassed that this had become necessary, and they had not told anyone, apart from having to supply the medical certificate to his employers, excusing him from work. She also volunteered the information that their daughter was not an easy person. She had held a number of jobs, but always seemed to cause trouble with other members of the staff, and was constantly moving on. So she asked her daughter what she meant by her question about her father. The daughter said, 'I know that Dad was exorcised at 5.30 pm last Monday afternoon, and I lost my power over people at the same time – and I want it back!'

I can understand that she may have inherited the Romany psychic powers from her father, but I have no explanation as to why they should have left her at the same moment as they left her father, when she was not even present at the time.

Using spiritual weapons

There was a particular occasion when I was very aware of the truth of Paul's words: 'The weapons we fight with are not the weapons of the world. On the contrary, they have divine power to demolish strongholds' (2 Corinthians 10:4).

The white witch

One day, I was contacted by a Baptist minister who was a member of a ministers' fraternal, which I attended. He knew that I had been involved in the deliverance ministry, and asked me if I would be willing to meet with him and a member of his congregation. In fact, it was the man's wife who was the member, but her husband accompanied her to a service occasionally. He had begun to act very strangely (I cannot recall the exact details, if I ever knew them). His wife had prevailed upon him to consult the Baptist minister, who believed that he might be demonised, although I doubt that he used that term in discussions with the man. It was agreed that I should meet with this man, the minister and one of the church deacons in the vestry of the Baptist church.

I cannot remember quite how I was introduced to this man, whom I will call Derek – possibly as a counsellor. I began to question him very gently about what he perceived to be the problem. He explained that he was involved in white witchcraft. He stressed that it was only 'white', and he used it only for the good and well-being of others; he had never had anything to do with black witchcraft. Here I would comment that in my experience, once you open the door to the occult, you cannot control what comes in, white or black. He was a pleasant and very reasonable man but, as we talked, his manner changed, and he really became rather rude. At first, he continued to speak quietly, but he told me that he really did not think I would be of any use to him at all because I didn't understand. Then he told me I was completely ignorant and knew nothing of witchcraft or its power; in fact, I was completely useless.

I realised that just as the spirits had put Eve into a trance and caused George to be unable to distinguish the words I was speaking, so the spirits in Derek were beginning to panic at my questioning, and their anger was being expressed through him. So I stopped my interrogation and suggested that we should pray. Derek was not too happy but somewhat reluctantly agreed. In my prayer, I brought Derek before the Lord and asked that he would deal with whatever had been causing him distress and set him free. Although this was very general, and far less direct than I would have chosen had Derek been more co-operative, it was sufficient to provoke a reaction in Derek, who began to cough and breathe heavily. I believe that some deliverance took place, but I was convinced that much more was needed. However, Derek stood up and proclaimed that he felt much better and that he had to leave. He thanked us all for our time, and that was that. I explained to my Baptist friend that I was by no means sure that Derek was clear, but we could not have held him against his will, and I left.

About three weeks later, my minister friend telephoned to say that Derek had returned, admitting that he was a great deal worse and requesting further help. We agreed a time, and again I went over to the church to meet with the same three. In view of what had happened before, I did not question Derek at all. I would have preferred to have got him to understand that his involvement in any form of witchcraft was wrong, and to repent of it before I began to minister, but I believed this would simply have stirred up the same belligerence he had shown before. So I went straight into it and, looking him straight in the eye, I said, 'I come in the name of the Lord Jesus Christ, and command every spirit contrary to the Holy Spirit of God to leave.'

The effect was immediate and dramatic. In the case of Eve, I have described how the spirits within her put her out cold, and she lay unmoving on the floor until I made the sign of the cross over her. With Derek it was the exact opposite. He rose out of his chair and came slowly and menacingly towards me, clenching his fists as though he intended to punch me. He was a tall, well-built man – far bigger than I – and I remember seeing, from the side of my eye, the Baptist minister and his deacon standing behind Derek, watching with interest what would happen.

It is surprising how many different thoughts can pass through the human brain, apparently at the same time. I remember thinking, 'Why don't they move forward with Derek, to intervene if he does try to hit me?' I was also thinking that I was wearing glasses, and wondered if I ought to remove them in case he broke them. But my overriding thought, which I am sure was put into my mind by the Holy Spirit, was that this was a spiritual battle, and however much my natural reaction was to raise my arm to ward off any blow, I must not do that. To remove my glasses or raise my arm would be to bring the conflict onto a human and physical basis; I knew it was important that I should rely solely on the power of the name of Jesus.

As he approached me, Derek said, 'You have no power over me! You have no power over me!' I held his eyes with mine and said, 'I stand in the name of Jesus, and at his name you must yield; come out now!' Derek came within about two feet of me and stopped, with his fist still clenched, reiterating, 'You have no power over me!' and I continued to look into his eyes, claiming the authority of the Lord Jesus Christ. Oh, what a struggle I had to keep my arm down; I believe had I raised it at all, he would have hit me. As it was, he took a step back, and then another and another, still protesting that I had no power over him. Of course, it wasn't truly Derek saying that; the spirit was using his voice. As he retreated further and further from me (and I remained where I was), the protestations had less and less conviction, and became more and more of a whine, rather like a bully whose bombast turns to complaint about being treated unfairly. Derek continued to retreat to the far wall of the room, with our eyes still locked. He slowly sank to the floor, where he assumed a foetal position, shut his eyes and then *he* raised his arm, as though to shield a blow from *me*, still saying, 'You have no power over me!' But it was in disillusionment, as though what he now meant was, 'You *shouldn't* have any power over me.'

I remained exactly where I had been throughout the whole episode and said, without raising my voice particularly, 'At the

name of Jesus every knee must bow, in heaven and on earth
and under the earth. You are subject to him and must go now.'
Suddenly, Derek got up from the floor with a great roar, drew
back his arm and smashed his clenched fist into the panel of a
door with such violence that it caused it to crack. Then his
whole demeanour changed; his body relaxed, and he shook
himself as though he were recovering from a blow on the
head, and asked, 'What's happened to my hand?' He had been
totally oblivious to all that had been going on and could recall
nothing of it.

Before I left, we had a prayer of blessing, and I was concerned that they should get Derek to a doctor to look at his
hand and, as the Baptist minister was responsible for his
ongoing pastoral care, I left it to him to warn Derek of the
dangers of getting involved with any form of witchcraft.
When I next met with the Baptist minister, I enquired about
Derek, and apparently all was well.

That happened many years ago, but recently I was talking
with a friend, who said, 'I met someone last week who says he
knows you.' It turned out to be Derek. 'He says that you exorcised him years ago and he has had no more trouble.' It is good
to hear that the name of Jesus still has its ancient power.

General principles

In recounting these various cases, I have described many of the
different methods I have felt it right to use according to the situations which faced me. Nevertheless, it may be helpful to
share some general principles.

I have already spoken of the power of the name of Jesus and
of the word of Scripture. I may well ask the person to repeat
the name 'Jesus' slowly and with meaning, concentrating their

thoughts not simply on the name but on the person. Evil spirits cannot tolerate the name of Jesus. Also, they hate praise. To speak aloud the worship and praise of God – not only by the patient, who in severe cases may be unable even to speak the name of Jesus, but by all who are present – will often bring a strong reaction.

It can be very beneficial to quote specific texts which relate to the presenting problems. Thus, if the person refers to oppressive darkness, it is sensible to speak out words of light: 'God said, "Let there be light"', 'I come in the name of Jesus, who proclaimed, "I am the Light of the world." ' Sometimes, the patient will react physically to the word 'light', as though they have actually been struck by a blow to the head. If there is a spirit of death, then I refer to the claim of Jesus to be 'the Resurrection and the Life'. Similarly, feelings of hatred should be countered by texts which refer to love: 'God so loved the world . . .' Lies should be countered by truth, rejection by acceptance ('accepted in the beloved') and so on.

As well as the spoken word, I have encountered cases where to hold the Bible over the head of the afflicted person can cause a strong reaction, which helps to dislodge the evil spirit. The vessels used in holy communion can have a similar effect. I have a small set, which I use for communion of the sick in their homes. To bring this, still in its case, near to a person who is demonised may cause distress (although it is the person who *exhibits* the distress, it is actually the evil spirit within them which causes it), but I have never known the person themselves to ask me to remove either the Bible or the communion vessels. Having said this, I must stress that in many cases, holding the Bible or the communion vessels over a patient may provoke no response at all. As I constantly reiterate, every case is unique.

It can be very helpful to ask the person to look into my eyes; this is actually so that I may look into theirs. They may find this very difficult indeed, not only because socially it can be unnerving to stare into the eyes of someone else for anything but the briefest time, but because it seems that any evil spirit which is present may be using the physical eyes of the afflicted person. Sometimes, as I have looked into a patient's eyes, I have had a sensation which I find it difficult to describe. Normally when you do this, however briefly, you get a response; we speak of someone's 'smiling' eyes, or of 'anger blazing' in their eyes. But with a demonised person it may be that 'nothing' is there. Logically, that statement is foolish – how can 'nothing' be anywhere? All I can say is that when this happens nothing comes back to you; there is no response. It is like a fathomless well, or infinity; your 'looking' goes on and on and meets with nothing. However, I have found that this experience is helpful, not only because it may be an indication that an evil spirit is present, but also it helps to dislodge it. It may be, and of course I cannot prove this, that the spirit looks into my eyes and sees something of the person of Jesus. If this sounds boastful, I would say only that Jesus promised his followers that he would be in them: 'On that day you will realise that I am in my Father, and you are in me, and I am in you' (John 14:20).

I am the first to admit that I am not worthy, but I do believe what he has said, and from experience I have discovered that if I act on my belief, evil spirits know it also. As I say, the person may find it difficult to hold my eyes with theirs, and usually, while I am doing this, I will kneel in front of them while they sit, so that our eyes are level. Even so, they may drop their eyes and look at the floor, or simply close them. If this happens, I explain to them that if *they* find it difficult, the spirit hates it, and I encourage them to persevere.

I have discovered that the greatest difficulty in deliverance is to get started; once the spirits begin to manifest, it gets easier. Very often the person will begin to cough, to retch or even to vomit. To be specific, this is not like a tummy upset, where the whole contents of the stomach may be brought up, but it may well be advisable to have a small bowl available and a box of tissues. I do not know that spirits, which by definition are non-corporeal, have a particular area of the human body where they congregate or dwell, but certainly very often they seem to rise from the stomach. With regard to the Holy Spirit, the Bible often equates this with the breath of God and with the wind, so it is not surprising if evil spirits, as they leave a person, should also be associated with breath or wind. The patient may well be able to sense and indicate where it seems to be, rising up their windpipe. Often, it seems to get caught in the throat; perhaps this is its last attempt to stay within the body, because once it rises higher than this I have never yet known it to stay in the mouth; it is always expelled. Very often the manifestation of its leaving will not be as strong as even a cough – just a gentle sigh, or a yawn.

Bill Subritzky (*Demons Defeated,* Sovereign World 1996), a New Zealand layman and lawyer with great experience of deliverance, believes the spirits may depart from any orifice of the body, including the ears and eyes. I cannot speak to that, but certainly I can confirm that they seem to leave by the mouth or nose, causing the person to cough, sigh or sneeze. On one occasion, the patient produced a considerable amount of white foam. Subritzky claims that these are not the spirits themselves, but 'nests' in which they have dwelt within the person. I do not know how he can be so certain, but I accept that the foam is not the spirits themselves. Subritzky also advocates asking the person to take a slow, deep breath and then exhale, as though panting, to encourage the spirits to move.

In order to dislodge the spirits, I may speak out biblical texts which seem to be appropriate, and remind them that they are in the presence of the risen Lord Jesus, or read a passage of Scripture which relates how Jesus drove out a spirit in his own earthly ministry. I have, on occasions, said a prayer of blessing over a glass of water and asked the person to swallow some. I have also anointed their forehead with oil, making the sign of the cross. I may pray that the Holy Spirit would enter into the depths of the person's being, bringing the light of Christ to shine upon any spirit of darkness within them.

There is a question as to whether it is appropriate to lay on hands in the ministry of deliverance. Corrie Ten Boom, the Dutch saint placed in a concentration camp by the Nazis during the Second World War for assisting Jews, warned against this very strongly, in the belief that it might enable the evil spirit to pass from the patient to the minister, and pointing out that while Jesus frequently touched a person in need of healing, there is no record of him doing this to anyone who was demonised. I have certainly laid my hands on their head when praying the Holy Spirit *into* a person to whom I am ministering, but I am wary about laying on hands to call the evil spirit out.

Here let me say, in passing, that I have heard of exorcists who call upon the evil spirit to come out of the afflicted person and into themselves. There is no biblical warrant for this, and I believe it is extremely dangerous and foolish, and should never be practised by a Christian (or anyone else for that matter).

Another stratagem I frequently employ is to make the sign

of the cross over the person and then take the 'sword of the spirit' – the word of God – quoting a verse such as, 'If the Son sets you free, you will be free indeed' (John 8:36); then I say, slowly and deliberately, 'I take authority over every spirit contrary to the Holy Spirit, and I cut you off from any and every source of power. I set the name (blood, victory) of Jesus between you and the powers of darkness. You are on your own now; your time has come to leave this person, be subject to the Lord Jesus, and never again enter any living being. You are to come out now.' Sometimes I will repeat the word 'cut' slowly and deliberately: 'I cut, cut, cut every link and cord which holds you to this child of God (or person). You can no longer stay; in the name of Jesus Christ, you must leave.'

When a spirit seems to be particularly stubborn, I have found it may be useful to speak in tongues. Sometimes this seems to have no effect whatever, but on occasions it has provoked a dramatic response. Of course, I have no idea what I am actually saying, but I believe that the Holy Spirit, who knows exactly what is needed, is interceding through me, and this has proved the key which dislodges the spirit, and we can begin to move forward.

Once a spirit has been dislodged and expelled, as I say, the deliverance gets progressively easier. I have already explained that these spirits hunt in packs, and they exhibit the personalities of bullies – strong and belligerent when they are together, but rapidly showing signs of panic once their numbers decrease. A device that I have discovered to be particularly effective, once a number of spirits have been expelled, is to speak to those that remain as though they are indeed bullies: 'Look around you; you will see that many of your fellows have already gone, and now you must leave, too. Quickly now, in the name of Jesus – out.' I am aware that it may sound naïve and fanciful to speak of them in this way; I can say only that in my experience time and again it works, and I am more than prepared to be regarded as a fool if the afflicted person is set free.

In the past, I have assumed that it was important to deliver the person totally before sending them home, or to ensure that they were in the care of some competent person. In the case of Eve, who, it will be remembered, had actually gone through a satanic marriage and invited spirits to enter her, I believe this was such a serious case that full-time care was essential. However, in the great majority of cases, the person has not invited the spirits to enter or, at least, had not intended to invite them (as in the case of Derek, who thought he was confining his activities to white witchcraft). Now, very often I will explain to the person that a great deal of deliverance has already taken place (usually they are very well aware of this, and may assume that because they feel so very different they are entirely free). However, it may be that there is a residue left behind. If they walk with the Lord, consciously calling upon him and seeking to obey him, any spirits which still remain will find it far too uncomfortable, and will leave of their own accord. If they should be worried, then they are free to contact their parish priest (who normally will have been present throughout the session) and, if necessary, he can contact me. However, this is unlikely (I seek to bolster their own confidence in the Lord). Should they experience any manifestations similar to what has just been happening (e.g. the sense of something rising up their windpipe), there is no need to panic; they are entitled to say quietly, 'You know you are subject to Jesus,' or 'You know I belong to Jesus and you have no right to stay; leave now.'

I must relate one case which completely baffled me, and which backs up the suggestions of the Christian Deliverance Study Group regarding family stress.

The teenager with the cut arm

A neighbouring vicar telephoned to tell me of a mother and daughter who had come to him, troubled by some strange and frightening events connected to the daughter. I arranged to call to see them, although unfortunately it had to be at a time when the vicar could not accompany me, and I took a lay minister with me.

At the home, several members of the family were there: the mother and daughter (whom I will call Beth), aged 16, an older daughter, who was serving in the forces but happened to be home at the time, and the mother's husband, who was Beth's stepfather. The mother worked as a ward assistant in the local hospital, and a few days before, Beth had turned up at the hospital to see her mother, who was on a night shift, very frightened and with a cut on her arm. She claimed that the cut had just 'appeared'; it was not deep, but it was a few inches long. I was well aware that teenagers can do all sorts of things to attract attention, and she might well have inflicted the wound on herself with a razor blade. She also spoke of other strange manifestations.

As I questioned them, Beth admitted that she had been involved in some forms of occult activity in her bedroom. She wasn't deeply into it, but had tried to call upon spirit powers to give her influence over others. Of course, this was stupid and dangerous, but it was little more than teenage curiosity and experiment. However, she complained of feeling that something was seeking to get at her. A few days before my visit, another cut had appeared on her arm, but this time the mother was present and had actually witnessed it happening. There was no razor blade or other implement; the cut just appeared. There was no sign of it by the time of my visit. Although part of me was sceptical, there was no doubt that the mother, Beth and particularly the older sister, were very upset and frightened.

As I continued my questions and began to explain the dangers of dabbling in the occult, the stepfather began to interject, first with questions and then with his own explanations. I hope I am not being uncharitable in saying he was the sort of person who is ignorant of a subject but who nevertheless is all too ready to express a view: 'With all respect to you, Vicar, let me tell you what I think . . .' His presence certainly wasn't helpful, because he constantly diverted everyone's attention from Beth and her problems to himself. What became abundantly clear, however, was that there was serious tension between him and Beth. In his comments he would frequently throw in remarks such as, 'Of course, I don't know what she gets up to in the evenings. I can't believe it's anything good.'

There had been some manifestations in Beth's bedroom and I promised to pray there before I left, but first I wanted to pray with Beth herself. As soon as I began, the family dog, which, after having greeted us on our arrival, had been lying quietly in the adjoining kitchen, suddenly began to growl and it became very disturbed. When I stopped praying and resumed normal conversation, the dog was quiet, but if I prayed and ministered it began to growl again. This led me to believe that there probably was some form of occult activity involved. However, Beth herself did not react in any way, and she said that she was not aware of anything at all happening as I prayed. She and her mother took me to her bedroom, where I prayed in the manner which I have already explained, after

Beth had repented of her attempted occult activities. Then my friend and I left.

Within days, they contacted their vicar again and explained that there had been further manifestations, which had caused extreme distress to all three women. So we arranged a meeting the following Sunday afternoon in the church with the three of them, plus the vicar, the vicar of another church nearby, a lay Christian and myself. The mother herself commented that the stepfather would not be there, because she had recognised that his presence had not been helpful on the previous occasion.

There is no point in me detailing either the things that had been happening or the form of ministry I used that afternoon, because it would add nothing to the other cases I have recorded. Suffice it to say that I used just about every approach I could think of, but nothing had any effect. Beth manifested nothing and was aware of nothing happening. After a considerable time of ministry, I had to admit defeat.

Some days later, the vicar called on the family in their home and began to unravel something of the tension that existed, particularly between Beth and her stepfather, and this apparently helped greatly.

As I say, the case baffled me. There is no doubt that the three women were very distressed, and I find it difficult to believe that the whole thing was made up. There was the strange behaviour of the dog, which pointed to some form of occult activity, and Beth admitted to dabbling in it – and how could the cut on her arm suddenly appear while her mother watched it happen? However, it seems that this was a case where the whole thing centred round the difficult relationship between Beth and her stepfather, which adds weight to the suggestion of the Christian Deliverance Study Group that it is such tension which can lie behind some of the problems of those who seek exorcism.

Let me close this chapter by recounting two other cases.

The woman with a spirit of death

A Baptist minister asked me if I would accompany him to the home of a man who had called on him regarding his wife. Neither of them was a member of his church, but he was the nearest Christian minister, and the man had sought his help. The minister gave me such background as the man had shared with him, but when we arrived at the home I asked for the two of them to give me the full details again.

They had been married only about a month, but almost from the beginning the husband had been woken in the night by his wife, whom I will call June, attacking him. She was unable to give any reason for this, and said that she certainly did not wish to do so. In the course of my questioning, it came out that June used a Ouija board, which was upstairs in their bedroom. I explained that using the board and asking questions of a spirit was dangerous and was expressly against the commands of God (I read to them Deuteronomy 18:10–13), and that by doing this she was inviting spirits to guide her, and very likely these had used the opportunity to take up residence within her. I strongly recommended that they should get rid of the board immediately and, rather than leave it somewhere for another person to find, that they should burn it. The husband agreed to do this at once, and went upstairs to get the board to take it out into the garden. Although June had also agreed to this, as he brought it into the room where we were gathered, on his way to the kitchen and thence to the garden, she cried out, 'No! No!' and came across the room as though to hit me. The husband and the Baptist minister restrained her, and the former said, 'That is exactly what I have been trying to tell you she does to me.' June recovered herself rapidly, and he went out into the garden. A little later, he returned to say that he had set fire to the board.

After further questioning and discussion, I suggested that I should minister to June, and she readily agreed. It was not long before she manifested demonisation, and it took the form of her speaking in a deeper voice than she had been using, and her words became slower and slower, while her head seemed to become heavier and heavier, as though she were falling asleep even as she spoke. I had met up with this phenomenon on at least one previous occasion, when it had transpired that there was a spirit of death within the person. I stopped the ministry and, using her name so that I would establish full contact with her and not the spirit, I said, 'June, forgive me for asking you, but will you tell me something – have you ever had an abortion?' but she denied it.

I returned to the ministry and spoke directly to the spirit of death, so that it would know I was aware of its presence. However, although once again it manifested itself in the slow, heavy speech, it did not leave her. I used just about every technique I have described, but I was unable to get it to come out. In the end I had to admit defeat and, after saying a prayer of blessing, the Baptist minister and I left them.

Almost exactly a year later, I received a telephone call from June. She wasn't sure that I would recall our previous meeting, and explained the circumstances. She said that she was still oppressed by the spirit(s) and asked if I would be willing to meet with her again. She was still in the same house, but her husband had left, and the marriage was over. Then she said, 'Do you remember that you asked me if I had ever had an abortion? I told you I hadn't. Actually, I had – some time before, but we were only just married, and I hadn't told my husband about it. I just couldn't bring myself to admit it in front of him.'

Looking back, I regret that I had not spoken to June without her husband being present. However, I am not sure what else I could have done. As the Baptist minister and I did not have a woman assistant with us, it would have been wrong for us to meet with June without the husband being there; certainly we could not have attempted any form of deliverance, and it would have aroused his suspicions had I asked him to go into another room while June spoke to me. The question of whether she had had an abortion just arose in my mind, and I had asked it.

During the intervening time, the Baptist minister had moved elsewhere, so I arranged an appointment when I could call on June, together with appropriate assistants. When we met, I explained to June that the abortion, putting her unborn baby to death, was probably what was enabling the spirit of death to hook into her. I led June into her repentance, confession and absolution. I then turned to the deliverance and commanded the spirit to leave, which it did without any trouble or delay. June was very aware of the immediate difference within her.

I tried to link her to a Christian fellowship in her area, and told her that she was free to contact me again if she needed further help. She never did, and I have no idea what happened to her.

I report this final case because it contains incidents which are not present in any of those recorded already.

The two friends and the budgerigar

The incumbent of a parish some eight miles or so away telephoned to ask me to help with a woman who had complained of feeling she was under attack from forces which she could neither identify nor explain. He had met with her and was at a loss to know what to do. He wondered if she was indeed under some form of occult oppression and asked if I would be willing to see her, together with himself. We arranged a suitable appointment for one Thursday afternoon.

I called at his vicarage, and he took me to a home which was set in a large council estate in his parish. I was disconcerted to find that, although she had agreed to the appointment, the house was full of a number of people – many of them children. It was difficult to find a room where the three of us could be quiet. In the end, we sat on the stairs to talk. I must admit that I was rather annoyed to have set aside the time, when I had a busy parish of my own to look after, and travelled some distance, only to find that she was remarkably offhand about the whole thing. With hindsight, I suppose I should have refused to do anything at all then, and either simply let the matter be or arranged another appointment, this time at the church. However, I have learned from experience that some people are really very deeply frightened, but seek to cover this up by trying to carry on in as normal a manner as they can. Some live in shared accommodation and are not used to any privacy, and it is all too easy for people to feel that the church has had no time for them when they have plucked up the courage to call on the clergy – which in itself may open them to ridicule from their neighbours. So, in spite of the far less than ideal situation, I felt I should at least explore whether there was anything I could do. In spite of my questions, the woman, whom I will call Sylvia, was unable to explain with any clarity what had been troubling her. She spoke of a presence around her or 'attached' to her, which was unpleasant. She could not say when she had first become aware of it, but it had grown in intensity over recent days, which is why she had sought help.

To be honest, I doubted that there was any occult influence involved; it sounded to me much more likely to be a psychological problem. But sitting there on the stairs was not conducive to further questioning, and I reasoned that it would be best to pray in a manner that might allay Sylvia's fears if they were simply in her mind and tell her to contact her vicar again if the problem should continue (when, of course, he and I would have the opportunity to make more careful arrangements). So I prayed that the peace of God would be upon her and, in the name of Christ, I set her free from any spirit contrary to the Holy Spirit, but I did not specifically command any spirits to come out from her, because I did not believe there were any involved. She did not manifest any indication of anything departing from her, so I laid my hand on her head to bless her, and then her vicar and I departed. Outside, we commented on the difficult situation we had faced, and went our separate ways.

The next day, Friday, was my day off and, as we usually did, my wife and I got out of the parish. It is also the day that the weekly church papers are published. On that particular Friday, there was a report of an exorcism that had gone badly wrong. A group of Christians, which included a clergyman, had attempted to deliver someone from an evil spirit. It had been a spontaneous decision to go down that path, and neither the bishop nor his appointed adviser regarding the occult had been consulted. Far from improving the situation, the patient became worse, and a complaint had been made, which inevitably led to the bishop having to intervene and severely reprimand the priest and the group who were involved. The national press had got hold of the story, and now the church papers were commenting on the case in some depth. It made lurid reading, and it was just the scenario that I have always dreaded. Although I seek to take the greatest care, there is always the danger that someone involved in witchcraft or Satanism may attempt deliberately to set up a false exorcism in order to discredit anyone whom they see as a threat to themselves or their beliefs, quite apart from the distress which can be caused if deliverance is attempted on a person who is, in fact, suffering from some mental disorder. Not only does it discredit the individuals involved in the disaster, but it discredits the church, and simply adds grist to the mill of those, particularly within the medical profession, who ridicule the claim that evil spirits do exist.

That night, shortly after I had gone to bed, the bedside telephone rang. It was the vicar of the parish I had visited the day before. Apparently, a close friend of Sylvia had had a sudden and drastic change in personality. The husband was desperately concerned and, on checking with others, he had discovered that the change had happened at the very time I was praying that Sylvia should be set free from any spirit that was bothering her. The strange thing was that his wife, whom I will call Sue, had not been with us at the time, but was in her own home, in a different part of the estate, over half a mile away. Because of the connection, the husband had approached the vicar for help. In explaining the situation to me, the vicar mentioned that Sue was a lapsed Roman Catholic. The story of the disastrous exorcism reported in that day's church press was still vivid in my mind, and I was not at all keen to get further involved, so I suggested that they should contact their local Roman Catholic priest. However, the vicar said that they had already refused to do this; apparently, Sylvia had been helped by my ministrations and, in view of what they saw as the link, they had specifically asked for me to see Sue also. The husband was absolutely beside himself with worry.

Reluctantly, I agreed to come out to him. At that moment, the vicar asked me to hold the phone while he checked something. Shortly afterwards, he came on the line to say that all the lights in his house had gone out. He had gone to the front gate, and seen that the electricity in the whole area had failed.

I dressed and drove the eight miles to his vicarage. It was very eerie, as I drew near, to find all the streets in complete darkness. He got into my car and directed me to the house of Sue and her husband. They had been able to find only the stub of one candle, which was all the light available. I began to question them, or rather to question the husband, because Sue was incapable of coherent speech. She was acting like someone on drugs – a zombie. Her husband told me that she had never displayed such symptoms in the whole of her life, and repeated what I had already heard, that this had happened suddenly the previous afternoon, at the exact time I had prayed with Sylvia. He had returned from work to find her with another friend, who had told him that she had witnessed this sudden change in Sue. He had gone off to work again that Friday morning, asking a neighbour to keep an eye on Sue, hoping that she would be better as the day wore on, but she wasn't.

He then mentioned that after my prayer with her, Sylvia had felt totally different and free. In fact, she had come round to see Sue, and was at that moment asleep in bed, upstairs in Sue's house. (I was having enough problems trying to find out just what had happened to Sue, without asking why Sylvia had not returned to her own home, but had calmly gone to bed in her friend's house, when they were so obviously distressed.)

The whole thing was getting more and more curious, and I was becoming more and more apprehensive. I could picture the headlines in the national press! I would have liked to consult with Sue's doctor, but it was almost midnight. Her husband assured me that she was not taking any medication, and was not under the doctor. He said, 'You helped Sylvia; please help Sue now. I cannot go through another night with her like this.'

At that moment, the candle gave out, and we were left in darkness. The husband said, 'Wait a moment, I've had an idea; let me get my bike.' I must digress here to say that in spite of all my apprehension, I could see the funny side of the situation. I was in a house in someone else's parish, in complete darkness, with Sylvia, whom to my utter surprise I had apparently exorcised without realising it, in bed upstairs for some unknown reason instead of being in her own home, and this distraught husband had gone to get his bike. In fact, it was a motor bike. In order to get it into his narrow kitchen, he had to raise the front and balance it on the back wheel. He then lowered it so that it pointed from the kitchen into the living room, where we were, and switched on the headlight, which gave some illumination.

So there were the four of us in the room: Sue, her husband, the vicar and myself. I felt I had to cover myself as much as I could, and I said to the husband, 'I will minister to your wife, but if there is anything I do that you are not completely happy about, you must speak out and tell me to stop. I do not want you to say afterwards that you were concerned at any of my actions. My colleague here will also witness what happens.' The husband said simply, 'Please, just do all you can; I want my wife back.'

I turned to Sue and addressed whatever spirit was in her,

commanding that it should be subject to Jesus and was to leave her. At that moment, I was startled by a noise behind me. There was a budgerigar in a cage, which, in the darkness, I had not noticed before. It went berserk! It was squawking and throwing itself against the bars of its cage. I have already mentioned that dogs and cats are often a good indication of some occult presence, but I had never before realised that budgerigars are also similarly affected.

I find it difficult to describe my state of mind at that time. It really was a frightening situation. I felt I had not been fully in control of this case from the outset. I had not believed that Sylvia was really demonised, and I had prayed little more than a blessing on her. I did not understand why Sue should have been affected, but clearly she was, and now she was not in a fit state to answer the questions I would have liked to ask. There was the added difficulty of having to operate in near darkness, which in itself made it all the more eerie. In addition, I was apprehensive because of the report I had read that day of the exorcism which had gone badly wrong. I have explained that it is important that the person ministering deliverance should have total confidence in the power and presence of Jesus and in the guidance of the Holy Spirit, so I tried to put my fears and apprehension to one side. In fact, part of me was very calm, and I felt I was standing back and analysing what was going on. With regard to the budgerigar, I was interested to see if it was coincidence, or related to the deliverance, so I stopped the ministry for a moment; the bird quietened down. As soon as I resumed the deliverance, it again went mad – I thought it was bound to injure itself; its behaviour was so violent. I remember thinking, 'This will be interesting when I report it to the bishop.' Then I actually laughed, because the sheer mad humour of the whole situation hit me, but I am not sure what effect this had on the husband, hearing me laugh while his wife was in such a state.

I mention all this in some detail because I truly believe the Lord was in it. I was so churned up that I needed to relax and renew my trust in him rather than myself, and being able to stand back and see the funny side of it calmed me and restored my sense of authority. As I continued to command the spirit to leave Sue, I walked round behind the chair where she was sitting. I held my closed Bible over her head. She was sitting bent forward, with her hands over her face, and I am convinced that she could not see what I was doing. I even checked that there was no mirror which might reflect my actions. Her head moved away from wherever I held the Bible over her. It was quite a violent movement, as when someone is moving their head away from a wasp buzzing near them. I removed the Bible, and her head remained still; I held it over her again, and her head dodged to get away from it, wherever I placed it. All this encouraged me and built up my confidence that we were gaining the victory.

I will not repeat the details of the techniques I used, which I have already described as being helpful in ministering deliverance. In a comparatively short time – five or ten minutes – Sue coughed violently, then sighed, and her head fell back gently against the back of the chair (and the budgerigar immediately became quiet). However, at the moment Sue sighed, there was a loud scream from upstairs. I checked with Sue to find out how she was; she was speaking normally with her husband, totally transformed. So the vicar and I then went upstairs and called out to Sylvia to ask if she was all right. She called us into the room where she was in bed, and when I asked her what had happened, she explained that the nearest she could come to explaining it was that she had been dozing and something had suddenly pushed past her, as though it were in a hurry to get somewhere else. She assured us she was all right. We returned to the living room and found Sue a little weary but, according to her grateful husband, fully restored. The vicar agreed to contact them the next day, to ensure that all was well, and I took him to his house and drove home to mine. There was no further problem.

That case is unusual in many ways, but what particularly intrigued me is that the spirit troubling Sylvia should travel some half a mile to infest her friend. It will be recalled that in the case of George, his daughter lost her own 'spirit power' when he was delivered of the spirit infesting him, but with them I can understand the hereditary link. With Sylvia and Sue, there was no family tie at all, and I have no explanation for what happened.

6
Odds and Ends

I have come into contact with other areas of the occult, but of which I have little experience.

Curses

Occasionally, people have come to me saying that they believe they have been cursed by someone, either in words alone or sometimes by pins being stuck into a doll-like representation of themselves as a curse is uttered. It may be that they have been told by the person issuing the curse that he or she has done this.

Although I will question the patient carefully, whatever information this yields I find it sensible always to pray with them, because it is impossible to prove that no curse has in fact been uttered, and the simple act of ministering to them in this way may give the relief and reassurance that they need. Also, unlike attempting to cast out a spirit when there is not one, it causes no harm.

I have used a variety of methods in dealing with curses.

Originally, on the advice of a more experienced colleague, I would proclaim in the course of my prayer that any curse uttered against the patient should rebound on the person who uttered it, rather as though a reflective shield were being erected around them, and on the principle that a word once uttered, like an arrow shot from a bow, cannot be called back. Scripture takes very seriously the power of a word expressed, especially if it is expressed with an intent. It is like a bomb which has been primed. It will explode; all you can do is choose the place where it does so. However, Jesus stated: 'Bless those who curse you' (Luke 6:28).

Perhaps in the spiritual realm, blessing neutralises a curse, on the principle laid down by Paul: 'Do not be overcome by evil, but overcome evil with good' (Romans 12:21). So I try to get the person involved to be willing to agree with me to bless the one who, they believe, has uttered the curse. Certainly in the course of ministering I will quote the verse: 'Christ redeemed us from the curse of the law by becoming a curse for us, for it is written: "Cursed is everyone who is hung on a tree"' (Galatians 3:13). I will pray along the lines that just as Jesus took our sin upon him on the cross, so we lay any curse which may have been uttered on him also. I am aware, of course, that here Paul was speaking specifically of the Law rather than any individual curses which may be uttered. However, on the cross, Jesus took all the hate and evil of the world and absorbed it and neutralised its sting.

Those to whom I have ministered in this way express their thanks, but I am never sure whether anything has actually changed or, if it has, just what has happened.

Ley-lines

This is a complicated subject, and certainly I am no expert in it. It covers a very wide range of interests, and those who study the matter differ as to how wide the research should be. Some would relate 'crop circles' and the sighting of UFOs to ley-lines; for others, it should be confined to the study of certain ancient sites. For me to attempt to go into greater detail would confuse myself, let alone anyone else. Basically, it has been discovered that certain prehistoric sites, such as stone circles (e.g. Stonehenge), barrows and other burial mounds, 'camps' and buildings are set in surprising alignment. Very often these sites are a considerable distance from each other and hidden by hills, so the exact alignment could not have been made by the naked eye. The question is, therefore, how were those who developed them able to place them in such exact geometric patterns, when they had none of today's equipment available?

The suggestion is that there are certain lines which, certainly in one popular theory, carry unseen forces – 'earth forces'. Perhaps they are magnetic paths or some other source of power which cannot be measured by any scientific instruments so far invented, but which could be picked up or tapped into by the unsophisticated but intuitive human mind. What, for instance, is the explanation of the 'gift' of dowsing?

Dom Robert Petitpierre had made some study of the phenomenon, and believed that there was certainly some force involved, and where two or more ley-lines crossed, they produced a greater degree of power. Very often, a pagan site of worship or magic had been set up at such a place. When St Augustine came to Britain, he had the idea of building churches on such sites. Today, Christians would probably seek a site anywhere other than one of pagan worship. However, the brilliance of his plan was that the ancient sites were now Christianised, and if others wanted to practise the ancient pagan rites, it was they who had to find a new site and start all over again.

I heard Dom Robert recount a story of how he was called in by the vicar of an ancient church built on the site of an even earlier one. Apparently, there were a number of paranormal disturbances occurring at the church. Dom Robert did some research, and discovered that this was indeed a place where ley-lines met, and which had been used years back for pagan worship. On questioning the priest, it became clear that he had a very liberal approach to the Christian faith in regard to both Scripture and traditional doctrine. Dom Robert believed that this had been instrumental in allowing the 'earth forces' of the ley-lines, which had been used in the pagan rites, to reassert themselves. He held a service of holy communion 'with special intent' in the church, and told the vicar, 'Get your faith sorted out, and do the job for which you were ordained.' Apparently, the occult manifestations ceased.

I have no idea as to whether ley-lines do exist or, if they do, whether there is any power associated with them. Certainly many people refute the concept, dismissing it, together with aliens and UFOs. The only reason I mention the matter here is because I am aware that some paranormal and witchcraft groups do believe that ley-lines exist, and they seek to use the power they believe is there in practising their craft. I have been told that the source of the power arises in South East Asia, travels along ley-lines through Europe and enters the UK somewhere near Southampton, before dividing into a whole network of lines spreading across the land. Whether or not this is true, I believe it is wrong and dangerous to seek to gain power from such a source, and the case of Derek and his white witchcraft illustrates this.

Trinkets and idols

I am sometimes asked about carvings and artefacts brought into homes from abroad, especially from Africa, India, South America and the Caribbean, as to whether they can have any occult influence. Certainly I know of missionaries who would hold that there is a demon behind every idol used for worship. That is something which is extremely difficult to prove, of course. I know personally of families where some disaster has occurred after some carving from overseas has been brought into a home, but who can say whether it is simple coincidence or if there is any connection between the two? For myself, if I knew that an article had been used in the worship of some foreign God, I would be very wary of bringing it into my home. I am mindful of what happened in the case of June, and her attempt to attack me when I recommended that she and her husband should burn the Ouija board she had been using. I do believe that there can be strong evil spiritual forces involved.

Sometimes the artefacts are very ugly and frightening. I realise that often shields and masks are deliberately made in this way in order to scare the enemy. (I assume they were effective, because they certainly scare me!) If someone is concerned about some such carving I may well suggest that they do get rid of it because the doubt they have in their mind may well be sufficient to cause distress, whether or not there is really any occult influence involved. With regard to ordinary articles brought from abroad, it may well be sensible to pray a simple prayer of sanctification to ensure that they are 'clean'. There are some very beautiful carvings that are simply expressions of the culture of another nation, and it would be sad to throw them out. It is similar to what I have written about some areas of alternative medicine; we should not throw the baby out with the bath water.

Can towns and cities be under a dominating spirit?

Again, this is difficult to prove. I know Christian leaders who are convinced that there can be spirits over a town which affect its inhabitants. Of course, we all know that some cities pervade an air of welcome or of joy, and others are oppressive and foreboding, and we can speak loosely of 'the spirit' of the place, but that does not necessarily mean that we believe there is actually an occult spirit or demon there.

Very often, on entering some ancient church, I feel that the prayers of the faithful down the years have somehow soaked into the walls of the building. I know that this can be dismissed as a psychological reaction to the sense of peace and the presence of 'holy' items, like the altar and the Bible on the lectern, and that may be so, but for me that does not fully explain it; there is a sense of the presence of the Lord himself. I can understand, therefore, how a place which was the site of some horrific tragedy, perhaps the concentration camps in Germany, can carry into the future a spirit of darkness and despair. After all, what do we think we are doing when we consecrate a church, or even a burial ground, setting it apart for a holy use? Is it an empty gesture, or do we believe that something happens? And if we don't believe it, why do we continue to do it?

In Chapter 4 we looked at the possibility of spiritual powers ruling over nations. I know of no reference in Scripture to cities being controlled or influenced by evil spirits, but there are those that are influenced by evil men: Sodom and Babylon, for instance. The Bible exhorts us to 'pray for the peace of Jerusalem', and so, whatever the truth of the matter, surely it can only be good to pray God's presence and blessing on a town or city.

Epilogue

Shortly after I was ordained, I was called upon to act as crematorium duty chaplain for a day. The role entailed taking those funerals at which, for one good reason or another, the priest of the parish involved was unable to officiate. It was a busy crematorium in south-east London, and it could handle over 20 funerals a day. That day, I took seven of them. It was difficult because I had not previously met the bereaved families, and I knew nothing of the deceased. I remember arriving home late that afternoon very depressed, and saying to my wife, 'Everyone is dying.'

This book is about the paranormal and so, of course, it is full of stories relating to the cleansing of places and the deliverance of people from evil spirits, and readers may be left with the impression that these events are much more frequent than in fact they are. They relate to a period of almost 30 years and, having been on the bishop's advisory group for the whole diocese during that time, I have been far more involved with them than the vast majority of parish priests. Of the cases referred to me, far more required counselling or medical treatment than deliverance. Nevertheless, it is an area that needs to be taken seriously, and the dangers of dabbling in the occult need to be broadcast more clearly than they are.

As I have already said, it is not an area of ministry I seek or enjoy, and when I am called upon to enter into it, I usually have a feeling of apprehension – as several of the cases I have reported illustrate. I believe that is good because, aware of my weakness, it prevents me from putting any trust in my own wisdom or abilities; I am compelled to depend upon the Lord. However, if the church, and particularly the established church of the land, is unwilling to offer help to those oppressed (or demonised, to use the scriptural term), where can they go, other than to spiritists and witches? I believe this is what Jesus described as inviting Satan to cast out Satan.

However, there is one great bonus, which was summed up by the curate who was present and assisted at the case of Eve, the student who had entered into a marriage ceremony with Satan. At the time, he had been ordained less than three months. Afterwards, he said to me, 'I am so glad that at the very beginning of my ministry I have witnessed for myself the power of the name of Jesus.' If ever I am tempted to doubt the great truths of the Christian faith, I remind myself of what I have experienced and seen; the victory of Jesus in the lives of men and women bound by Satan. Christianity is not a philosophy; it is not even, at heart, a religion. It is a relationship with Jesus, who is as alive today as ever he has been.

Index

Other books in the Ministry Guides
series . . . to be published in 2002

The Prophet's Notebook
by Barry Kissell

The first in an exciting new series consisting of five
'Notebooks', each covering a different ministry listed
by Paul in Ephesians 4. *The Prophet's Notebook* will help
prophets to recognise their gifts and use them to build
up the people of God.

The Evangelist's Notebook
by John Peters

John Peters believes we need to make radical changes
in the way we evangelise. Why would non-Christians
want to come to church if they can't understand what's
going on and if we can't explain to them, in everyday
language, what we believe?

The Apostle's Notebook
by Mike Breen

Mike Breen looks at what the Bible has to say and
comes to some surprising and challenging conclusions
on the role of the apostle in today's church.

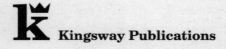

Kingsway Publications